Sweetmeats

Karim Khan

methuen | drama

LONDON • NEW YORK • OXFORD • NEW DELHI • SYDNEY

METHUEN DRAMA
Bloomsbury Publishing Plc, 50 Bedford Square, London, WC1B 3DP, UK
Bloomsbury Publishing Inc, 1359 Broadway, New York, NY 10018, USA
Bloomsbury Publishing Ireland, 29 Earlsfort Terrace, Dublin 2, D02 AY28, Ireland

BLOOMSBURY, METHUEN DRAMA and the Methuen Drama logo are trademarks of Bloomsbury Publishing Plc.

First published in Great Britain 2026

Cover design: Art Direction by Kelly Thurston

Cover image: Photography by Courtney Phillip

A catalogue record for this book is available from the British Library.

A catalog record for this book is available from the Library of Congress.

ISBN: PB: 978-1-3506-0335-6
ePDF: 978-1-3506-0337-0
eBook: 978-1-3506-0336-3

Series: Modern Plays

Typeset by Mark Heslington Ltd, Scarborough, North Yorkshire

For product safety related questions contact productsafety@bloomsbury.com.

To find out more about our authors and books visit www.bloomsbury.com and sign up for our newsletters.

Sweetmeats
By Karim Khan

A Bush Theatre and Tara Theatre co-production

Cast

Hema	Shobu Kapoor
Liaquat	Rehan Sheikh
Liaquat's wife	voiced by Sudha Bhuchar

Creative Team

Writer	Karim Khan
Director	Natasha Kathi-Chandra
Set & Costume Designer	Aldo Vázquez
Movement Director	Mateus Daniel
Lighting Designer	Simeon Miller
Sound Designer	Hugh Sheehan
Composer	Amrit Kaur Lohia
Costume Supervisor	Malena Arcucci
Casting Director	Chloe Blake
Voice Coach	Gurkiran Kaur
Production Manager	Chloe Stally-Gibson
Company Stage Manager	Ella Godbold-Holmes
Assistant Stage Manager	Wang Shuyin
RADA Stage Management Placement	Rachel Wilkinson
Set Builder	Paul Grace
Production Electrician	Kevin James

For Bush Theatre

Lead Producer	Nikita Karia
Lead Dramaturg	Olivia Poglio-Nwabali
Marketing Campaign Lead	Kelly Thurston
Press Manager	Martin Shippen
Technical & Buildings Manager	Jamie Haigh
Technician	Jonno Strutt
Schools Project Lead & Community Producer	Holly Smith

For Tara Theatre

General Manager & Producer	Ceri Lothian
Associate Director	Gavin Joseph
Head of Marketing	Becca Pratt
PR	Bread & Butter PR

Special thanks to Helen Jeffreys, Sudha Bhuchar, Adil Akram, Ansuman Biswas, Gurnesha Bola, Paul Grace, Maariyah Sharjil, Kiln Theatre and the Young Vic.

This premiere of *Sweetmeats* is dedicated in memory of Abdul Shayek, Artistic Director & joint CEO of Tara Theatre (2020–3) – a visionary and dreamer who dared to envision and fight for a more equitable world.

Developed with early development support from Rifco Theatre Company. Generously supported by Cockayne Grants for the Arts and Royal Victoria Hall Foundation.

The London Community Foundation

CAST

Shobu Kapoor | Hema

In a career spanning over three decades, Shobu Kapoor has played a range of characters across theatre, television, film, radio as well as voiceover roles.

Recent film and television credits include: *Wicker* (Escape Plan); *Quarter Life, The Dark Tower pilot* (both Amazon); *I Am Not Alice Bell* (Clapperboard); lead in feature film *Polite Society* (Focus/Working Title); *Bridgerton 2* (Netflix); *Three Little Birds, DI Ray, Unforgotten* (all ITV); *We Are Lady Parts 1 & 2* (Channel 4); *A Discovery of Witches S3, I Hate Suzie* (both Sky); *Four Weddings and a Funeral* (Hulu); *Krypton* (Syfy/DC); *The Cleaner, The Split, Bend It Like Beckham, EastEnders, Citizen Khan S1–5* (all BBC); *Whitstable Pearl* (Acorn).

Her theatre credits include: *Genesis Inc, What Fatima Did* (both Hampstead); *Dinner With Saddam* (Menier); *Lotus Beauty* (Gate); *Yerma* (Arcola).

Rehan Sheikh | Liaquat

Rehan Sheikh is a London-born actor, writer and filmmaker active in Britain and Pakistan since the 1990s.

Known for his work in Pakistani drama serials, film and television, Rehan began his theatre journey with running a South Asian youth theatre group in South London whilst studying for his drama degree. He worked with Tamasha Theatre Company on eleven productions, including: *Women of the Dust; Shaft of Sunlight; A Tainted Dawn; Ghost Dancing; Balti Kings; A Fine Balance.*

Rehan won Best Actor at Kara Film Festival 2005 and Best Supporting Actor 2015 Hum Awards. He has also written and directed films *Mohabat Ki Pehli Kahani, Azad, Surprise,* and is a poet, vlogger and teacher.

Additional theatre credits include: *Silence* (Donmar/Tara); *Indian wants the Bronx* (Young Vic); *Mary Mary* (Karachi); *Death and the Maiden* (Rafi Peer Festival).

TV credits include: fifty-plus serials including *The Castle, Zard Paton Ka Bann, Sadqay Tumharay, Aghosh, Inkar, The Bill.*

Web series include: *The Pink Shirt.*

Radio credits include: *Sidharta; Crazy Night; The Good Person of Ajmer; Lysistrata; The Dancing Girls of Lahore; The Bounty Hunter.*

Film credits include: *Manto; Actor in Law; Silent Water; Azad* and the upcoming *Apnas.*

CREATIVE TEAM

Karim Khan | Writer

Karim Khan (he/him) is an award-winning playwright and screenwriter from Oxford. His show *Brown Boys Swim* sold out at the Edinburgh Festival Fringe in 2022, transferred to Soho Theatre, toured nationally and was optioned by A24. He is currently developing new work with the Royal Court, RSC, National Theatre and Soho Theatre.

Past stage credits include *Before the Millennium* (Old Fire Station), *Corrosive* (Pegasus Theatre), *Beyond Shame* (Derby Theatre) and *Orange Juice* (Pleasance). He has written episodes for *All Creatures Great and Small*, winning Best Debut at the Edinburgh TV Festival in 2023.

He is preparing to direct his debut short film with Amazon Prime and NFTS. In 2022, he was awarded the inaugural Pillars Artist Fellowship, supported by Riz Ahmed's Left Handed Films, and sponsored by Netflix and Amazon. Karim is an MA Screenwriting graduate (2019) from the National Film and Television School with a scholarship from Toledo Productions and Channel 4.

Natasha Kathi-Chandra | Director

Natasha Kathi-Chandra (she/her) is an international theatre director and writer based in London, UK, and Hyderabad, India. She was appointed Artistic Director and Joint CEO of Tara Theatre in February 2024 after having worked as Associate Director there since 2022.

As Associate Director for Tara Theatre she was instrumental in the organisation's Theatre of Sanctuary Award and Business Innovation Award in Wandsworth in 2023. She also conceptualised and launched Tara Theatre's flagship Young Company programme.

Natasha's directing credits include:

For Tara Theatre: *I Dream of Theresa May; DNA*; *Artists Make Space* (nominated for the International Award at The Stage Awards 2023).

As Director: *It Kind of Looks Like a Doughnut* (Pleasance, Nottingham Playhouse, Wolverhampton Arena); *4 Stages* (Bread & Roses, Offie nominated); *Om Shanti F*ck* (Arcola); *Sad About the Cows* (Tristan Bates); *The Infinite Line Between Dating and Dying* (Etcetera).

As Associate Director: *East Is East* (Birmingham Rep, National, Chichester); *AMMA* (Tara).

As Assistant Director: *The Woods* (Royal Court); *The House of In Between* (Stratford East).

Other directing credits: *The Lion King*, *Les Misérables*, *The Crucible*, *Checkmate* (2008–12, India).

Aldo Vázquez | Set & Costume Designer

Aldo Vázquez is a Mexican set and costume designer based in the UK. He trained at Bristol Old Vic Theatre School with an MA in Theatre Design, and a BA in Visual Arts from the UNAM/ENAP, Mexico City. He has worked both in Mexico and the UK collaborating with international directors and actors from Argentina, Canada, China, Mexico, USA, UK and Switzerland.

Recent credits include: *Romeo and Juliet* (Edinburgh); *The Beautiful Future Is Coming*, *Cheeky Little Brown* (Bristol Old Vic); *In Search of Goldoni* (UK tour); *Falkland Sound*, *First Encounters: The Tempest* (Royal Shakespeare Company); *Blood Wedding*, *Our House*, *Caresses*, *Pish!*, *The Suicide*, *Boy* (Bristol School of Acting); *Mephisto*, *Icarus*, *Robin & Marian*, *Fefu and Friends*, *Pericles* (Bristol Old Vic Theatre School); *Until I Find You* (Ad Infinitum); *The Boys Are Kissing*, *Moreno* (Theatre503). As Associate Costume Designer: *Why Am I So Single?* (West End).

Simeon Miller | Lighting Designer

Recent credits include: *Orphans*, *The Poison Belt* (both Jermyn Street); *A Christmas Carol*, *An Adventure* (Bolton Octagon); *Marriage Material*, *The Sun Shines for Everyone*, *The Mob Reformers* (all Lyric Hammersmith); *Of Mice and Men* (Derby); *The Jungle Book* (Theatre by the Lake); *Brace Brace* (Royal Court); *Follow the Signs* (Soho); *After Sex* (Arcola); *Brief Encounter* (Royal Exchange); *Silence* (UK tour); *Cowbois* (RSC & Royal Court); *Pass It On*, *As We Face the Sun* (both Bush); *The Book of Will* (Queen's Theatre Hornchurch, Bolton Octagon); *Ruckus* (Southwark); *Jekyll and Hyde* (Derby, Queen's Theatre Hornchurch); *Project Dictator* (New Diorama); *Metamorphoses* (Globe); and *High Rise eState of Mind* (UK tour).

Hugh Sheehan | Sound Designer

Hugh Sheehan is a composer, sound designer, writer and audio producer from Birmingham. Now based in London after spending ten years living in Helsinki, Hugh makes music, theatre and audio programmes. Much of his practice explores questions of gender and sexuality, desire and shame, assimilation and radicalism.

Hugh has worked internationally as a composer and sound designer for theatre with directors including Roxy Cook, Natasha Kathi-Chandra, Josh Roche, Gabriella Bird, Ned Bennett and Christa Harris. As a musician he has performed and been commissioned by ensembles around Europe and North America.

Hugh's work as an audio producer includes the award-winning 5-part narrative audio documentary series *Criminally Queer: The Bolton 7* (dubbed 'mind-bending' and 'a staggering tale' by *The Guardian* and a 'sad, startling story skilfully unraveled' by *The Sunday Times*) as well as The Louis Theroux Podcast, BBC Radio 4's Profile and Factory International's Dream Space amongst others.

Amrit Kaur Lohia | Composer

Born and raised in Tottenham, Amrit Kaur Lohia is a singer-songwriter, Sarangi player and composer, described as 'the place where Punjabi folk meets Aretha soul' by *OZY* magazine.

Named a BBC Music Introducing artist and praised by Rick Rubin for her live performances, she has commanded the stages of Glastonbury Festival, The Jazz Cafe, The Barbican, Jaipur Literature Festival in India and the UN General Assembly with the Bob Marley family.

Having honed her craft from touring internationally since the age of fourteen and inspired by her studies in History at SOAS, University of London, and work with Off West End theatres in London, Amrit's music brings the heart of North Indian musical and storytelling traditions together with the grit of modern jazz, blues and soul.

Supported by Arts Council England, she will be releasing an album dedicated to her late sister, a musical experience encompassing grief, compassion, self-redemption and joy.

Mateus Daniel | Movement Director

Mateus Daniel is a movement director, choreographer and BBTA nominee from south London. He has built a love and curiosity for telling stories physically that express themes of culture, change and transitions, and has used his experiences within dance and theatre to influence his lyrical style. His work can be seen on various leading UK stages, magazines and films and his personal projects thematically take on a melodramatic, gothic perspective.

Movement director credits include: *Passion Fruit* (New Diorama); *Human Nurture* (Theatre Centre/tour); *Chicken Burger and Chips* (Brixton House); *The Boys Are Kissing* (Theatre503); *Vardy v Rooney: The Wagatha Christie Trial* (Ambassador); *Our Eyes Look to God* (Festival d'Aix-en Provence); *What I Hear I Keep, I'll Burn the Ocean/For You* (both Talawa); *As We Face the Sun*, *Communion* (both Bush); *TERRA XYZ* (Wonderland magazine); *TRIBE* (Young Vic); *Stranger Things: The First Shadow* (Phoenix); *No More Mr Nice Guy* (Broadway/Bristol Old Vic); *Vitamin D* (Soho); *Purgatory* (Donmar); *B*tch Boxer* (Watford Palace); *a practical guide on how to save the world when no one f***ing else is...* (Tara); *Spectacle of the Surreal* (V&A); *How to Win Against History* (Bristol Old Vic); *Safe Space* (Chichester).

Malena Arcucci | Costume Supervisor

Born and raised in Buenos Aires, Malena Arcucci is a theatre designer and costume supervisor based in London. She is co-artistic director of Mariana Malena Theatre Company.

Design credits include: *When You Pass Over My Tomb* (Arcola); *Super Chefs* (UK tour); *Strangers Like Me* (NT Connect, Hackney Shed); *The Bit Players* (Southwark); *Friday Night Love Poem* (Zoo Venues); *Playing Latinx* (Summerhall); *La Llorona* (Dance City Newcastle); *The Two of Us* (Theatre Deli); and various productions in Buenos Aires, Argentina.

Associate designer credits include: *Falkland Sound* (Royal Shakespeare Company); *Dear Elizabeth* (Gate); *Chiaroscuro*, *House of Ife* (both Bush); *Thebes Land* (Arcola).

Costume supervisor credits include: *The Empress*, *As You Like It* and *The Tempest* (Royal Shakespeare Company).

Chloe Blake | Casting Director

As casting director, theatre credits include: *Loot*, *Handbagged*, *The Turn of the Screw* (all Queen's Theatre Hornchurch); *Toto Kerblammo!*, *Odd and the Frost Giants*, *Huddle*, *The Odyssey*, *The Wolf, the Duck and the Mouse*, *The Three Billy Goats Gruff* (all Unicorn); *Warehouse* (WiseCrack); *I Dream of Theresa May* (Tara); *Jekyll and Hyde*, *Shut Up I'm Dreaming*, *Hamlet* (school productions for the National).

As casting associate, theatre credits include: *The Importance of Being Earnest*, *Till the Stars Come Down*, *The Other Place*, *Nye*, *The Effect*, *Blues for an Alabama Sky* (National).

Chloe was Children's Casting Associate for *Standing at the Sky's Edge* (also West End), *Till the Stars Come Down* and *Small Island*, and provided additional casting for *Kerry Jackson*, all at the National.

Screen casting director credits include: *Divine Origins*, *The Algorithm of Loss*, *Mordik* and *Satisfaction*.

Chloe Stally-Gibson | Production Manager

Chloe is a freelance production manager and former associate artist of Zoo Co Theatre Company and ChewBoy Productions.

Her recent work includes: *Not Your Superwoman*, *Tender*, *This Might Not Be It, Insane Asylum Seekers* (all Bush); *Shifters* (Bush & Duke of York's); *Punch*, *A Face in the Crowd* (Young Vic); *Perfect Show for Rachel* (Barbican); *Playhouse Creatures* (JCTP); *Silence* (Tara).

Ella Godbold-Holmes | Company Stage Manager

Ella is a freelance company stage manager who has worked on a variety of productions ranging from West End to community-based projects.

Assistant stage manager credits include: *The Woman In Black* (West End).

Company stage manager credits include: *Dismissed* (Soho); *Bacon* (Edinburgh Festival Fringe); *The Time Machine: A Comedy* (UK tour); *Vitamin D* (Soho); *Pirates Love Underpants* (Leicester Curve); *Fatherland* (Hampstead); *Fireside Tales* (Punchdrunk Enrichment).

Ella is incredibly excited to work with both the Bush Theatre and Tara Theatre for the first time in her career. Huge thanks and love, as always, to her partner and her family, for their unending support.

Wang Shuyin | Assistant Stage Manager

Wang Shuyin is a stage manager and a writer who holds an MA Writing from the University of Warwick. Shuyin is passionate about shining the spotlight on the Global Majority, particularly ESEA communities in theatre.

Selected credits include: *Private View*, *Ugly Sisters* (both Soho); *Woo Woolf* (Cockpit); *Brown Girl Noise* revival (Riverside); *Pop Off, Michelangelo!* (Underbelly, George Square); *Permission*, *DNA* (both Tara); *King James* (Hampstead); *Pins and Needles*, *Two Strangers (Carry a Cake Across New York)* (both Kiln); *The End*, *Communion*, *The Cord* (all Bush); *Bat Night Market* (LIFT).

TARA THEATRE

For over four decades, Tara Theatre has supported the emergence of generations of South Asian performers, writers, directors, musicians and choreographers, and toured extensively both nationally and internationally. Artistic Director Natasha Kathi-Chandra continues this work, with Tara Theatre continuing its legacy of creating innovative, politically charged theatre, harnessing the power of co-creation.

Our work explores the complexities of our world through a South Asian lens, championing South Asian voices and artists, identifying new narratives, new ideas and new forms. Tara Theatre creates exceptional, innovative and politically charged theatre for now.

As the longest-running global majority-led theatre Tara Theatre is driving change within the UK theatre landscape, addressing the lack of diversity and representation and challenging our industry. Tara Theatre is a contemporary and democratic space, a centre for a wide-ranging community of artists and audiences locally, nationally and internationally. Tara Theatre believes everyone we work with is an artist and has an important and creative voice to be amplified, whether they are part of our local community, younger creatives, emerging talents, or established professionals.

Outside of Wandsworth, Tara Theatre works across the UK and internationally, with a focus on cities with large South Asian diaspora communities, including Greater Manchester, Leicester, Coventry, Birmingham, Derby and Leeds. Internationally, we are focused on cities within the South Asian region, as well as cities in other regions with large South Asian diaspora communities.

taratheatre.com

Staff

Artistic Director & Joint CEO	Natasha Kathi-Chandra
Executive Director & Joint CEO	Alys Beider
General Manager & Producer	Ceri Lothian
Senior Producer	Neena Shea
Associate Director	Gavin Joseph
Head of Marketing	Becca Pratt
Marketing Officer	Amal Abdi
Administrator	Shahreen Vayani
Senior Technician	Patrick McAneny
Fundraising Consultant	Sylvain Malburet

Bush Theatre

We make theatre for London. Now.

For over 50 years the Bush Theatre has been a world-famous home for new plays and an internationally renowned champion of playwrights.

Combining ambitious artistic programming with meaningful community engagement work and industry leading talent development schemes, the Bush Theatre champions and supports unheard voices to develop the artists and audiences of the future.

Since opening in 1972 the Bush has produced more than 500 ground-breaking premieres of new plays, developing an enviable reputation for its acclaimed productions nationally and internationally.

They have nurtured the careers of writers including James Graham, Lucy Kirkwood, Temi Wilkey, Jonathan Harvey and Jack Thorne. Recent successes include Tyrell Williams' *Red Pitch*, Benedict Lombe's *Shifters*, and Arinzé Kene's *Misty*. The Bush has won over 100 awards including the Olivier Award for Outstanding Achievement in Affliate Theatre for the past four years for Richard Gadd's *Baby Reindeer*, Igor Memic's *Old Bridge,* Waleed Akhtar's *The P Word* and Matilda Feyiṣayọ Ibini's *Sleepova*.

Located in the renovated old library on Uxbridge Road in the heart of Shepherd's Bush, the Bush Theatre continues to create a space where all communities can be part of its future and call the theatre home.

'The place to go for ground-breaking work as diverse as its audiences' EVENING STANDARD

bushtheatre.co.uk
@bushtheatre

Artistic Director & Co-CEO	Taio Lawson
Executive Director & Co-CEO	Angela Wachner
Outgoing Artistic Director	Lynette Linton
Outgoing Executive Director	Mimi Findlay
Associate Director	Katie Greenall
Executive & Operations Assistant	Deborah Bahi
Development Manager	Choi
Head of Development (maternity leave)	Jocelyn Cox
People & Culture Administrator	Dorothy Ekema-Walla
Finance Assistant	Lauren Francis
Technical & Buildings Manager	Jamie Haigh
Producer	Emma Halstead
Assistant Venue Manager	Rae Harm
Head of Finance	Neil Harris
Lead Producer	Nikita Karia
Box Office Supervisor	Paula Kramer
Community Producing Assistant	Joanne Leung
Event Sales Manager	Simon Pilling
Literary Manager & Lead Dramaturge	Olivia Poglio-Nwabali
Venue Manager (Theatre)	Ade Seriki
Press Manager	Martin Shippen
Head of Community	Holly Smith
Technician	Jonathan Strutt
Development Lead	Ines Tercio
Head of Marketing	Ed Theakston
Marketing Officer	Kelly Thurston
Marketing & Development Assistant	Amelia White
General Manager	Camille Wilhelm
Café Bar Manager	Wayne Wilson

DUTY MANAGERS
Sara Dawood & Jacob Meier

VENUE SUPERVISORS
Antony Baker, Adryne Caulder-James, Bo Leandro, Nzuzi Malemda, Chana Nardone & Asa Wooldridge.

VENUE ASSISTANTS
Emma Chatel, Pyerre Clarke, Georgia Fellows, Daniel Fesoom, Matias Hailu, Nzuzi Malemba, Ishani McGuire, Ed Mendoza, Dumo Mkweli, Carys Murray, Louis Nicholson, James Robertson, Manuel Ruis, Ali Shah, Eleanor Stock, Josie Watson, Nefertari Williams, Anna-May Wood & Yemi Yohannes.

Bush Theatre, 7 Uxbridge Road, London W12 8LJ
Box Office: 020 8743 5050 | Administration: 020 8743 3584
Email: info@bushtheatre.co.uk | bushtheatre.co.uk

THANK YOU

Our supporters make our work possible. Together, we're evolving the canon and creating a bolder, more diverse, and representative future for British theatre. We're so grateful to you all.

MAJOR DONORS
Charles Holloway OBE
Jim & Michelle Gibson
Rajeev Philip
Cathy & Tim Score
Susie Simkins
Jack Thorne
Gianni & Michael Alen-Buckley
Bhagat Sharma
Dame Emma Thompson
Joe Tinston & Amelia Knott

SHOOTING STARS
Jim & Michelle Gibson
Anthony Marraccino & Mariela Manso
Cathy & Tim Score
Susie Simkins

LONE STARS
Clyde Cooper
Adam Kenwright
Jim Marshall
Georgia Oetker

HANDFUL OF STARS
Charlie Bigham
Judy Bollinger
Richard & Sarah Clarke
Christopher delaMare
David des Jardins
Sue Fletcher
Thea Guest
Kate Hamer Ltd.
Elizabeth Jack
Simon & Katherine Johnson
Joanna Kennedy
Garry & Lorna Lawrence
Phyllida Lloyd & Kate Pakenham
Vivienne Lukey
Sam & Jim Murgatroyd
Mark & Anne Paterson
Nick & Annie Reid

RISING STARS
Elizabeth Beebe
Martin Blackburn
David Brooks
Catharine Browne
Anthony Chantry
Lauren Clancy
Caroline Clasen
Susan Cuff
Matthew Cushen
Anne-Hélène and Rafaël Biosse Duplan
Austin Erwin
Kim Evans
Mimi Findlay
Jack Gordon
Hugh & Sarah Grootenhuis
Sarah Harrison
Uzma Hasan
Lesley Hill & Russ Shaw
Davina & Malcolm Judelson
Katja van Koten
Mike Lewis
Lynette Linton
Tim & Deborah Maunder
Michael McCoy
Judy Mellor
Caro Millington
Rajiv Nathwani
Yoana Nenova
Stephen Pidcock
James St. Ville KC
Jan Topham
Kit & Anthony van Tulleken
Angela Wachner

CORPORATE SPONSORS
Biznography
Casting Pictures Ltd.
Nick Hern Books
S&P Global
The Agency

TRUSTS & FOUNDATIONS
Backstage Trust
Buffini Chao Foundation
Christina Smith Foundation
Daisy Trust
Esmée Fairbairn Foundation
The Foyle Foundation
Garfield Weston Foundation
Garrick Charitable Trust
The Golsoncott Foundation
Hammersmith United Charities
The Harold Hyam Wingate Foundation
Idlewild Trust
Jerwood Foundation
John Lyon's Charity
Martin Bowley Charitable Trust
Noël Coward Foundation
Royal Victorial Hall Foundation
The Thistle Trust

And all the donors who wish to remain anonymous.

If you are interested in finding out how to be involved, please visit **bushtheatre.co.uk/support-us** email **development@bushtheatre.co.uk** or call **020 8743 3584**.

Sweetmeats

The idea for *Sweetmeats* emerged in 2019, and I've been longing and yearning, just like its characters, to see it come to life ever since. The journey to this point has felt unpredictable and a lesson in faith and patience. Countless incredible people have witnessed its development, and have been fundamental champions of it, not least Abdul Shayek, the former Artistic Director of Tara Theatre. I remember when he first read the play in December 2022, he immediately knew he wanted to produce it. His verve and conviction are something that Natasha Kathi-Chandra, along with Tara Theatre, shares and holds in bucket loads. It's been a real honour and joy making this show with them.

In writing this play I wanted to shine a light on a generation of people we rarely see in our stories – our elders – and to make them the main characters of their own love story. We often see our elders as mothers, fathers and grandparents – foils to their younger counterparts, and yet we all know the dynamic and complex forces they truly are. Once young men and women who crossed continents to forge new lives, they became matriarchs and patriarchs of multigenerational families. I wanted to explore their desires, dreams, fears, and see them come of age, ultimately dare to grow and change – to fall in love.

Some of my favourite stories are about the brief connections that burn slowly and quietly between people – ones that feel delicate but intense, destined, irreversible and ephemeral. Love feels like one of the greatest inscrutable mysteries to me – something I'm still trying to fathom. Even in the past seven years in which *Sweetmeats* has been in my life, my feelings about it have changed, constantly flitting between hope and cynicism, and yet, whether I want to or not, I can't shake my indelible faith in the absolute possibility of a love that can and will transform people.

In a time of increasing friction and division, where acts of heinous cruelty feel tragically commonplace, it is vital that we are reminded of our capacity to love, and our need for it in our lives. Nothing affirms to me life's wonders more than seeing the quiet tenderness that lives between people who choose to love one another, despite knowing they'll one day lose them.

KK

My heartfelt thanks to:

Amaani Khan. Saeed Khan. Gurnesha Bola. Nic Wass. Ameet Chana. Pravesh Kumar. Lydia Rynne. Raagni Sharma. Shiv Jalota. Gitika Buttoo. Kash Arshad. Balisha Karra. Neil D'Souza. Sudha Bhuchar. Adil Akram. Madhav Sharma. Isma Almas. Qas Hamid. Deirdre O'Halloran. Lynette Linton. Daniel Bailey. Olivia Poglio-Nwabali. Taio Lawson. Kelly Knatchbull.

Aldo Vázquez. Simeon Miller. Mateus Daniel. Amrit Kaur Lohia. Hugh Sheehan. Malena Arcucci. Chloe Blake. Chloe Stally-Gibson. Ella Godbold-Holmes. Wang Shuyin. Ceri Lothian. Gavin Joseph.

NFTS Screenwriting Class '2019. Rifco Theatre Company. Bolton Octagon. NT Studios.

Abdul Shayek.

Natasha Kathi-Chandra. Shobu Kapoor. Rehan Sheikh.

Tara Theatre. Bush Theatre.

x

For Dedda

Notes

The play should flow, and scenes should spring from one another seamlessly – any transitions feeling as gentle as possible. Despite holding naturalistic markers, like the workshop, the play will in moments drift into an ethereal, transcendental space – almost a magical realm above reality.

Hema *and* **Liaquat** *are multilingual. Actors'/Director's discretion as to how present + pronounced an accent could be.*

– at the end of a line suggests the next line is an interruption

/ overlapping dialogue

. . . pauses, hesitation or contemplation

'beat' should be given the time appropriate to the moment.

Act One

One

School classroom. **Hema** *(Indian, 63) has a plaited ponytail, and a cardigan over her shalwar kameez. A dupatta shrouds her neck and reels to the seat beside her, occupying it. She busies herself with a bit of knitting before the workshop starts. She glances at her watch.*

Hema Mrs Radcliffe likes eating shortbread before she teaches diabetics to carb count. She snaps one finger in half and munches it like it's about to run away from her mouth. Crumbs spray on her sweater like ashes of a departed soul. Rest in peace. The other half she dips in her very milky tea, and I do not know which I feel more sorry for . . .

She sips her sugarless tea – she reduced it by half a teaspoon every week – practise what you preach – but now the sugarless tea is re-sugared with fragments of shortbread. The masses enter and disperse like crumbs on milky tea, she munches faster, wishing she started eating earlier, but it's too late, 'hello everybody', munch, 'take a seat', munch, swallow, there, gone. (*Sigh of relief.*)

I sit by nobody except the window. The wind is my friend. We speak to each other like reunited relatives. She wraps me in her sweet breeze, and I thank her for releasing me from the stuffiness of body odour and eau de toilette.

'Today we will look at ways you can manage your blood sugar levels by counting and monitoring your carbohydrate intake, by that I mean –'

Hema *sees* **Liaquat** *(Pakistani, 66) enter, in shalwar kameez – his belly sticks out. He ambles in with his sticky flip flops.*

Hema He strides in like a cock . . . amongst hens.

They are shocked he's committed the cardinal sin by sitting beside the scary Indian woman. But he's new, otherwise he would know better.

Liaquat *sits on* **Hema***'s dupatta. She yanks it out. He lifts his bottom for her to release it. He smiles.* **Hema** *doesn't.*

He has headphones on like a mindless teenager, and even though I don't care for what she has to say, I can't hear anything, because sounds seep out of it like maggots crawling from a cracked floorboard.

(*To Mrs Radcliffe.*) Sorry, can you repeat that, I didn't quite catch you . . . Nahi, it's just very difficult to hear you today.

Liaquat Did you forget your hearing aid?

Hema What was that?

Liaquat (*loud*) Hearing aid –

Hema Nahi, my hearing is perfect, first class, I just think, Mrs Radcliffe, if people don't want to pay attention and listen, what are they doing here? This isn't a nursing home.

Liaquat You can move closer if I'm a hindrance to you.

Hema Why should I move closer? I was here before you.

Liaquat Oh you want me to move closer?

Hema Or maybe you could just remove those pretty little headphones and listen to the woman, huh? Would you like someone to help you take them off?

Liaquat *removes his headphones and faces forward. A beat. Then he looks around. He tries to gain* **Hema***'s attention.*

Liaquat Hey!

Hema Kya?

Liaquat *searches his pockets. Looks through pieces of paper.*

Liaquat Is this the right place?

Hema Tum mera damaagh kharaab kar raho ho.

Liaquat Am I in the right place?

Hema How am I to know?

There's a pole fitness class over there – is that what you're looking for? –

Liaquat (*reads off paper*) Type 2 diabetes management course –

Hema You're in the right place. Now let's be quiet for the gori, bhai.

Liaquat Doctor referred me here three times –

Hema Three times?! –

Liaquat Three times! –

Hema And you show up now? –

Liaquat He said: Mr Aziz, you need to take this seriously otherwise your heart could stop, just like that, pop (*scares her*), but I say no, I won't let that happen, not on my watch. I will fight, I will go to these workshops, I will pay attention to everything they say, I will listen with every part of my soul, there's years in the old dog yet. Now, come on, let's listen to the woman.

They both face forward to listen. **Hema** *is peeved.*

Two

Outside school. Workshop has finished. **Hema** *is on her phone.* **Liaquat** *waits at the bus stop, standing close by, noticing* **Hema**.

Hema Beta, kahaan ho tum? Workshop khatam hogai. If you don't come in the next ten minutes, I'll walk back.

Hema *takes a flask from her bag. She unscrews the lid and pours bright pink Kashmiri chai into a cup.*

Liaquat Why do you speak English when you speak such wonderful Hindi? If I had a voice as sweet as yours, I'd never stop speaking the words of my motherland –

Hema My English might be good but I'm an Indian through and through.

Liaquat *sings the lyrics from 'Mera Joota Hai Japani'.*

Liaquat . . . phir bhi / dil hai hindustani.

Hema Dil hai Hindustani, spare us the whole song.

Liaquat Do you know what your voice sounded like when you drifted into your own tongue just then?

Hema You can return to your headphones now. Workshop khatam hogai –

Liaquat Hema Malini. That's who you sound like.

Hema How original of you –

Hema *peels her sticker off.* **Liaquat** *takes it and writes his name on it. He places it on his clothes.* **Hema** *takes her glasses to have a look.*

Hema Well done, you can write English.

Liaquat *Lia-quat* –

Hema Yes, I can read. You must learn to cross your tees.

Liaquat And do you know my namesake, Hema Malini? Guess. Go on.

Hema Some lafunga from the streets of Karachi?

Liaquat Nahi ji . . . Our first Prime Minister, Liaquat Ali Khan sahb, Allaah un kee magfirat karay.

Hema Oh. One of the men that tore through my country? What an honourable namesake.

Liaquat Wah. Is there a tiny Hindutva man inside you? Blink twice if you're in there.

Liaquat *steps aside jokingly.*

Hema Stop being so foolish.

Liaquat I thank Quaidi Azam and Liaquat sahb every day of my life for giving us Pakistan – what would be of us if we were still in your country, tauba tauba (*touching tips of ears*).

Hema Maybe ask all the people who would still be here – whose lives got snatched before their time, I mean both ours and yours.

Liaquat 'Ours and yours' yeh kya hai, yaar? We were the same . . . We are the same. Oh.

Hema What is it?

Liawuat (*sniffs*) Can I smell the chai of Kashmir?

Hema *screws the lid of the flask tightly, and places it away. She takes her knitting.*

Hema Who even calls it that?

Liaquat I can't remember the last time I sipped it.

Hema Does your wife not find you worthy of it?

Liaquat My wife isn't . . . she's not here.

Beat.

Hema I'm sorry.

Liaquat Koi baht nahi.

Beat.

Hema Would you like some? (*Expecting him to reject it.*)

Liaquat *considers, then nods.* **Hema** *is surprised.*

Hema Ek minute, I've put it away. (*Dishes out the flask.*)

Liaquat Teek hai, my bus won't be here for a while. Take your time.

Hema, *perturbed, unscrews the lid of the flask.* **Liaquat** *watches her.*

Liaquat Oooh beautifully pink, isn't it?

Hema I have nothing to pour it in.

Liaquat Pour it in the mug.

Hema I've used it.

Liaquat I don't mind.

Hema You'll catch my cold.

Liaquat I'll drink from the other side. Where did your lips press?

Hema You're a strange old man.

Liaquat Eh, less of the old, I'm still a child.

Hema Yes, you seem like one – I'll put it in the lid.

Liaquat The lid? The lid will only give me two mouthfuls.

Hema I can pour in more once you're finished. Here.

Liaquat *takes the lid.*

Hema Be careful. It'll burn your tongue.

Liaquat *shakes it in the air a little. Some spills.*

Liaquat It's cooler now, see.

Hema You've dropped half of it.

Liaquat Which leaves me one mouthful. Very well. Beggars can't be choosers. (*Almost as a prayer as he takes it to his mouth.*) She grips Kashmir til her knuckles turn white –

Hema What did you say? (**Liaquat** *drinks it like a shot. He spits it out.*) Didn't I say it was hot? I don't know why you're giving me those looks. Did I force you to drink it?

Hema *seeks the lid.*

Liaquat Tumhey sharam nahi aarahee hai?

Hema Kya?

Liaquat How can you make chai, Kashmiri chais of all chais, without a grain of sweet sugar?

Hema Forgotten you're diabetic eh? You got Alzheimer's as well?

Liaquat Me? You forgot to add sugar to chai. That's like me walking outside my house with . . . no clothes on.

Hema No it's not actually –

Liaquat It is –

Hema No, it's *not*. Look – maybe you need to go to a workshop where they teach you what diabetes actually means. No wonder you're on your headphones, bechara.

Liaquat *takes the lid and leaves.*

Hema Eh! Where are you going? Give me that. That's my lid.

Liaquat Some place will have sugar, little packets of sugar, three of them will suffice.

Hema I don't want sugar. I want my lid. Eh.

Liaquat You'll thank me in the end.

Hema No I won't.

Liaquat It'll be worth it.

Hema You'll get yourself run over. With my lid. Do you hear me? My lid. Can I please have my lid back?

Liaquat Just follow me, it'll be here somewhere.

Hema My son will be here any moment.

Liaquat There's a mithai shop just over there –

Hema No –

Liaquat It's only across the road. We can get a couple of ladoos –

Hema No –

Liaquat The ladoos are delicious –

Hema Honestly, can I –

Liaquat Don't worry, your son will see us.

Hema I don't want him to. I want my lid, please –

Liaquat *passes* **Hema** *the lid, it hits* **Hema***'s arm and spills on* **Hema**. **Hema** *winces in disgust.*

Hema Ugh.

Liaquat I'm sorry.

Liaquat *grabs a tissue from his pocket and tries to wipe it. She pushes away from him.*

Liaquat Oh my bus is here. See you next week. Khudafis.

Hema *watches him trail away in utter disbelief.*

Three

Liaquat *is at his home. He stares into the distance.*

Liaquat *has headphones in his ears. He has a tape player in his hand. We hear a young woman's voice from the 1970s. It's* **Liaquat***'s wife.*

Tape As' salam alaikum. Ammi, aap ki sehet kesey hai?

Liaquat Wa' alaikum as salaam . . .

Asma came with the kids. They're growing so quickly, *too* quickly. They brought something for me. An early birthday present. An alarm clock. Asma has set me two alarms. One for Fajr. And one for breakfast . . . 'You won't oversleep now, Dad' –

Liaquat *presses the tape as it resumes . . .*

Tape Kal hum ne ik film dekhee, us mein Amitabh Bachchan aur Shashi Kapoor thay. Tum ne dekhee hogee! Us ka naam kabhi kabhi thaa. Aur us ka song bahot piyara thaa, kabhi kabhi mere dil mein, mein ne Liaquat ke VHS pey tape karlee hai, aur tumhey dikhaoon gee'. I will show you. Tumhein bahot pasand aayga. You will love it so much.

A beat.

Liaquat *searches for the VHS tape.*

Liaquat Kabhi kabhi, Kabhi kabhi.

He can't find it anywhere.

Four

Hema *and* **Liaquat** *are at the workshop. They are some distance apart.*

Hema Mrs Radcliffe will finish the shortbread herself today, otherwise she'd have to take them home and share them with her family, who don't know how to share. They'd leave her half a biscuit and a packet of crumbs, greedy kuttai. So no, not this time. This time she will eat them alone.

To give her enough time, she creates a task to end the session. 'Why don't we get ourselves into pairs.' She's delighted that there's finally an even number with the addition of the 'irritating Pakistani man' who has a propensity to thieve other people's flask lids, and leave them soaking in their own chai. She no longer has to partner with the scary Indian woman, which means the scary Indian woman has to pair with –

Liaquat (*shouts across*) Do you have partner?

Hema Hahn.

Liaquat Kaun?

Hema Mrs Radcliffe.

Liaquat Mrs Radcliffe shortbread khaa rahee hai.

Liaquat *ambles to her.*

Hema Baghwaan mujhay himmat dey.

Liaquat So what do we have to do?

Hema You weren't listening?

Liaquat Gori speaks bahut bakwaaz. She needs to get to the point.

Hema We need to talk about how our one-to-one review went. (*Pause.*) Well, how did it go?

Liaquat Not bad, yours?

Hema You have to say more than that –

Liaquat My sugar's too high.

Hema You sound surprised.

Liaquat She says I need to lose this (*lifts belly*) –

Hema It's only advice.

Liaquat (*sighs with relief*) Thank God for that. I was getting so worried –

Hema But it's probably best you listen though.

Liaquat She said I shouldn't eat more than one small sugary food a week. And that should be my treat. That I should use sweeteners in my tea. For life!

Hema It's good you recognise the seriousness of this.

Liaquat What do I do with these?

Liaquat *brandishes a box of mithai.* **Hema** *is in shock.*

Hema Are you serious?

Liaquat *opens a box of bright yellow balls. Ladoos.*

Hema Put that away. You can't bring that out here.

Liaquat I brought a box last week, but you weren't here.

Hema Why?

Liaquat I don't know. You tell me –

Hema *Why* are you bringing mithai here?

Liaquat In case you brought sugarless Kashmiri chai again. I couldn't let you repeat that mistake now could I?

Hema So you ate it all yourself?

Liaquat Of course not. My grandson had one too. Um. Where is the chai? – (*glances for it*)

Hema You're still surprised your sugar's high?

Liaquat Here, take one.

Hema I have diabetes.

Liaquat (*sarcastic*) Really?

Hema You've got diabetes. We've both got diabetes. That's why we're here.

Liaquat Yet you miss last week, kya baaht hai?

Hema That could not be helped.

Liaquat Achaa? kya hua? . . . tum teek to ho na?

Hema My friend has gone back, to India. I went to see her one last time.

Liaquat Achaa. Chalo. (*Pushes the box forward.*) Live a little –

Hema No –

Liaquat Come on –

Hema Put it away –

Liaquat She's not looking. She's not.

Hema *tries her best to hide the box away.*

Hema (*quietly*) I haven't had mithai in . . . years.

Liaquat *is horrified.*

Liaquat Years?

Hema I want to live as long as I can.

Liaquat It makes me very, very sad to see you suffer this way.

Hema I'm not the one suffering.

Liaquat Very well, let me suffer in peace. Bismillah –

Liaquat *eats the ladoo.*

Hema You can't eat that in here!

Liaquat (*while munching*) I just did.

Hema Fine, I'll just watch you get in trouble then. We're supposed to be partners you know / What if I get in trouble for this?

Liaquat (*really enjoying it*) Mmmmmmm.

Hema Nice?

Liaquat Yes, you probably can't remember. I'll remind you what it tastes like –

Hema Spare me. I remember –

Liaquat (*examining ladoo in his hand*) It's crumbly, and sweet, and buttery and –

Hema It looks cheap to me. Greasy, and oily, and very bad for you –

Liaquat That it is.

Hema You're going to have another one, aren't you? (**Liaquat** *bites into another.*) Oh you just did. God!

Liaquat Well, you won't have one with me. One must eat alone.

Hema You'll give yourself a heart attack.

Liaquat Don't worry, I took extra tablet today.

Hema You'll be on insulin –

Liaquat A sharp scratch in the buttox, pfft, I've had worse –

Hema And what about when they chop off your big toe?

A beat. **Liaquat** *is taken aback. He drops the ladoo. Appetite gone.*

Hema Sorry.

Liaquat You have a dark imagination (*touches tips of ears*) tauba karro.

Hema Why are you here if you don't want to change?

A beat.

Liaquat Do you know the first time I really tasted this?

Hema The moment you were born?

Liaquat Bachphan meh my parents would treat sugar like gold dust. No matter how much I asked, they wouldn't let me try these things.

Hema They were wise.

Liaquat I would sit on my knees and watch rich men eat mithai and drink chai all day. Like a never-ending movie. It was like I was tasting it too. The first time I really tasted it was on my wedding. The mehndi.

Hema Achaa?

Liaquat Hahn, can you believe it? The ladies queued up beside a pyramid of ladoos, and one by one gave me a bite. Ooh, it was wonderful. The sugar, never-ending . . . (*recollecting*) but I had this sugar rush, and I began to feel tired, delirious, the sweetness of the ladoos wore off and my tongue became numb, my jaw ached . . . and I didn't want it anymore, but I kept biting, tearing the perfectly spherical orb . . . so in one sitting I tasted the very thing I dreamt of for so long, and felt sick of too. But you, you even abstained from sugar on your wedding day, didn't you?

Hema Of course not,

Liaquat Jhoot nahi bol.

Hema I ate sweet okay!

Liaquat Achaa?

Hema Yes. Who do you think I am?

Liaquat I struggle to believe it.

Hema Don't take this the wrong way, bhai sahb, but I never settled for those greasy things. I have standards. My husband went to so much trouble to get me these gorgeous little pieces of cardamom barfi.

Liaquat Elaichi? Oh hor –

Hema It's the best mithai in the world. Nothing even comes close. Nothing.

Liaquat *shakes his head with disbelief.*

Hema What? It is!

Liaquat Not as good as ladoo.

Hema Twice as good as ladoo, no, three times as good as that . . . gandhee cheez.

Liaquat No wonder you don't eat them. You lack taste when it comes to sweet delicacies. Try it. Come on, then make up your mind.

Hema Put it away.

Liaquat If this was cardamom barfi in my hand would you taste it?

Hema No, obviously not. You've touched it.

Liaquat But if I hadn't. Would you taste it?

Beat.

Hema If you had it right there, which you don't.

Liaquat But, if I did?

Beat.

Hema If it tasted like the ones my husband brought me –

Liaquat Hahn.

Hema You can't promise that.

Liaquat What if I could?

Hema That's impossible to promise –

Liaquat No it's not –

Hema He's dead.

Beat.

Liaquat Of course.

Hema I'm being silly. Ignore me.

Liaquat Nahi.

Hema You're talking about mithai.

Liaquat But it's what . . . he did for you that made it taste the way it did –

Hema Bakwaas.

Liaquat It's true –

Hema Maybe a small bite, enough to keep my levels stable.

Liaquat What?

Hema I'd maybe have a small bite . . . if I could.

Liaquat You'd make a return to mithai after all these years?

Hema Did you not hear me? I said a – small – bite.

The admittance even surprises **Hema**. **Liaquat** *takes this in.*

Five

Outside school. **Liaquat** *steps ahead.* **Hema** *stops still.*

Liaquat I always thought I would go back.

Hema We all did.

Liaquat Then life . . . life gets in your way. There's more people to think about.

Hema He wanted to wait til the children were old enough, then we would live the rest of our days there.

Liaquat Is that what you wanted?

Hema I came here for him.

Liaquat Then why are you still here?

Hema I can't –

Liaquat What's keeping you here?

A beat.

Hema What is there to go back to now?

Liaquat Mujhe pathai . . . You spend more years here than there, but still every part of me has the goan inside it. The village. Every time I go back, I think things will stay the same, but –

Hema They don't. Life changes everyone, bhai. Them and us. 'More years here than there', you're right (*processing it*) but everyone who sees me sees an old Indian woman.

Liaquat Not everyone . . .

Achaa, ready?

Hema I don't know.

Liaquat I'm certain they'll have it. They even have the chocolate and strawberry ones.

Hema My son will be here any moment now.

Liaquat We'll be back in time. He was late last time.

Hema Sometimes he's early.

Liaquat Well this time make him wait.

Hema He doesn't like waiting.

Liaquat Look how fast I walk. We'll be quick.

Hema I'm slower.

Liaquat I know how fast you run.

Hema When have you seen me run?

Liaquat Time is slipping from us –

Hema Across the road you say?

Liaquat Just there, look. Two minutes tops. You can take it home with you . . . or if you wait here, I could get it for you?

Hema Nahi. Why would you do that?

Liaquat Don't you want to taste it again? Your beloved barfi?

Hema I think I saw it.

Liaquat Kya?

Hema *moves.*

Hema His car. My son's car.

Liaquat Where?

Hema He's early. Didn't I say. That's him. Unpredictable.

Liaquat We can go another time . . . if you'd like to.

Hema He's getting out. I have to go. Sorry.

Liaquat Teek hai.

Liaquat *watches her go.* **Liaquat** *turns to the opposite direction.*

Hema *stops, turns.*

Hema I'll think about it.

See you next week.

Liaquat *smiles, nods.*

Six

Liaquat*'s home, kitchen.* **Liaquat** *plays the tape.*

Voice Mein ne itnay paraathay banai thay. Gobi ke parathay, keemay ke, Aaloo ke.

Sub kahey rahay thay ke kitnay mazay ke thay, they loved them, her koi mujhay bata raha which one was their favourite. Liaquat took a bite from each. And said nothing. Mujhay lagta hai us ke pasand ka ik bhee naheein thaa.

The tape ends. **Liaquat** *rewinds it. The last sentence replays. It's finished.*

Liaquat I loved each one of them. How did you not know that they were all my favourite, har ek.

He removes the tape from the cassette player, almost not sure what to do next.

Liaquat
I mix the flour, salt, oil in a mixing bowl.
I knead, I knead, I knead, I knead
Sticky dough glues to my fingers.
I roll it out and it sticks, it does-*n't* flat-*ten*.
I heat the tawa. Medium-high flame.
Like a little scared life.
It blazes bright, beautiful.
I place the paratha on the tawa.
A misshapen heart with a deep tear.
I drizzle ghee both sides.
I wait for it to puff. Breathe new life.
I wait . . .
For brown spots to grow.

I try to turn it over, but it just . . . sticks.
Like it'll stay there forever.

Blaring alarm scares **Liaquat**. *Smoke rises from it, almost otherworldly. He tries to waft it away, but it's hard. The alarm quietens completely.*

Seven

School classroom. **Hema** *and* **Liaquat** *are some distance apart.* **Hema** *occasionally glances at* **Liaquat** *almost intuitively, but she tries to return on course.*

Hema Mrs Radcliffe is on a diet. She's finally practising what she preaches. There's not a single shortbread finger in sight. To take her mind off the sweet food that she so desperately craves, she talks and talks and talks, she hasn't stopped for a breath bechari.

'We need to try and make changes to our food choices which are realistic and achievable so we can stick to them in the long term' blah, blah, blah damagh kharaab kari hai –

He's not even listening. His face hasn't turned this way once. I bet he's stuffed himself with so much food that it's sent him into a little doze, or . . . maybe the scary Indian woman has finally scared off the irritating Pakistani man.

Hema *packs up her things. She slowly walks towards him.*

Hema Bhai sahb! Teek ho?

Liaquat *looks up, removes his headphones.*

Liaquat Did I miss anything?

Hema What are you listening to? Gaana shaana?

Liaquat *packs away his headphones and cassette player.*

Liaquat You could call it that.

Hema Whose voice are you drowning your ears in?

Liaquat Mukesh.

Hema Mukesh?

Liaquat Hanji, aur Lata.

Hema Kaun sa?

Liaquat *sings a lyric from the song 'Kabhi Kabhi'.*

Hema Very good, very good. Listening to that is more important than health advice?

Liaquat What did I miss?

Hema She said we need to monitor the food we eat closely.

Liaquat Achaa?

Hema To make long-term healthier choices.

Liaquat Yes. I know this already –

Hema You do?

Liaquat Hahn –

Hema But you don't appear to have done much about it – (*Glances at stomach.*)

Liaquat (*notices* **Hema** *glance, he looks at it too*) Kya matlab?

Hema Kuch bhi nahi.

Liaquat Are you talking about my tid? Yes or no?

Hema Of course not.

Liaquat I saw you staring at it.

Hema I did no such thing.

Liaquat You're a terrible liar.

Liaquat *releases a smile to let* **Hema** *know he's teasing.*

Hema My grandson says the reason we hold more charbi is because the white man starved our people in famines . . . To control us.

Liaquat Achaa? Nothing's changed. Look at the gori.

Hema And so what happened was bit by bit all our bodies learnt how to hold fat, learnt how to deal with nothing inside.

Liaquat Very clever.

Hema But now we have everything at our fingertips – now the brown man eats like the white man, but the brown man does not have the white man's body.

Liaquat *processes this.* **Hema** *enjoys it.*

Liaquat So it's not my fault? My tid. My sugars. You know I thought this country gave me everything . . . It did give me everything. You're telling me iska daada naana –

Hema Nahi. Iska daada ka daada –

Liaquat Achaa? Iska daada ka daada is the reason we're here, and now she looks us up and down like . . . we did this to ourselves.

Hema It doesn't matter whose fault it is, we deal with the consequences. Who has time to grieve what was done to us? Will tears cure our diabetes?

A beat. **Liaquat** *ponders it, about to speak.*

Hema It wasn't a question, bhai. The answer is no.

Liaquat *takes this in.*

Hema I was telling my son about what his papa did for me . . . for our shaadi all those years ago. The cardamom barfi –

Liaquat You never told him before?

Hema (*shakes head*) It brought a smile to his face, and he started looking. He wanted it in time for Diwali, going from shop to shop all day long, but not a single shop had it. Maybe they don't make it anymore.

Liaquat Nahi, of course they do –

Hema I told him about the shop close to the school here, but he couldn't find it–

Liaquat He couldn't find it? The shop?

Hema Hahn. Did you make it up?

Liaquat That's a . . . slanderous, slanderous accusation. First you call me mota, now you call me a liar. Oh hor –

Hema I'm not calling you a liar, bhai. It was a question. He looked for it. He was devastated –

Liaquat I'm devastated for him. It's right there. Is he blind?

Hema Don't call my son blind!

Liaquat It was a question. Is he blind? –

Hema No of course he's not blind.

Liaquat (*to himself*) 'make it up' . . . why would I make it up? Did you not see the big shiny pieces of ladoo in my hand or are you beginning to doubt that as a figment of your imagination too?

Hema I can't be sure you got it from the same mithai shop which had the cardamom barfi –

Liaquat I bought it on my way here. Where else would I have got it from?

Hema I don't know. Tesco?

Liaquat Hai meri Allah. I'll prove to you it exists. You'll see it with your own eyes.

Have you got your things? Let me get my chappals. Ek mint.

Liaquat *looks for his flip flops. He finds one.*

Hema Maybe you could just tell me where it is, and then I'll tell him.

Liaquat Fikar nahi kar. I will show you where it is. You can take a few chungi de photos for him. I can't believe it. Accusing me of lies. Have you seen my chappal?

Hema *looks for it too.*

Hema There it is.

Liaquat Can you get it for me?

A beat. **Hema** *can't believe the cheek. She gets it.*

Liaquat Thank you. Chalo.

Hema Close by you say?

Liaquat I'll show you.

They are outside. They walk together. **Hema** *is a little awkward, self-conscious.*

Maintains distance. **Liaquat** *hums to Kabhi Kabhi. We should feel time pass, as they go on their way.*

Hema I didn't mean to accuse you of lying, bhai. It's just since I told him, paghal hogiya. He's desperate to find it before Diwali. He wants the little ones to have it – they never met their daada.

Liaquat But what about you?

Hema What about me?

Liaquat You'll get to taste it again, your beloved barfi.

Hema This isn't about me.

Liaquat *stops. Tired.* **Hema** *turns to him.*

Hema Bhai? Are you okay?

Liaquat *nods. He's shaky, dizzy.*

Hema Kya hua? Ao bettjao.

Liaquat *sits.* **Hema** *perches beside him.*

Liaquat I'm sorry. I don't know what's happening.

Hema You're shaking. Your sugar must be low. Where's your meter?

Liaquat It's at home.

Hema (*sarcastic*) Of course it's at home. Use mine.

Liaquat Nahi nahi –

Hema You must check your sugars, bhai.

Hema *searches her bag – and takes out a small testing meter bag. She gives it to him.*

Liaquat *takes out the test strips and fingerprick set. He tries to assemble it, but struggles. A little clueless.*

Hema Can I help?

Liaquat *reluctantly nods.*

Hema Idar doh.

Liaquat *passes* **Hema** *the blood strip and fingerprick test. She assembles it properly.*

Hema Give me your finger.

Liaquat Which one?

Hema Any. It doesn't matter.

Liaquat *looks at each of his fingers.*

Liaquat I don't know which one to choose. I like all of them.

Hema It won't hurt.

Liaquat *is still undecided.* **Hema** *quickly grabs a finger and pricks it.*

Liaquat *Owww!*

Hema Shhh.

The moment feels intimate between them.

Liaquat You said it won't hurt.

Hema It didn't hurt.

Liaquat How can you tell my pain? Are you psychic?

Hema Yes I am.

Hema *takes the strip and tries to fill it with blood. She presses it hard.*

Liaquat What are you doing? *Oouch*!

Hema It might not be enough,

Liaquat What? Don't say that.

Hema I might need to do it again.

Liaquat (*trying to remove his hand*) Nahi, nahi. You can't do it again.

Hema *lets go of* **Liaquat***'s hand.* **Liaquat** *sucks his finger.* **Hema** *places the testing strip into the meter.*

Liaquat I think . . . I think you enjoy seeing me in pain.

Hema You might not be wrong.

Liaquat Bechara Liaquat –

Hema It's low.

Liaquat Low?

Hema 3.4. You need to eat a sweet snack.

Liaquat We're on our way to get mithai, chal –

Hema No, no. Right now. You need something right now.

Liaquat It's just across the road.

Hema How long will it take?

Liaquat Ten. Fifteen minutes.

Hema That isn't just 'across the road'. More walking will only lower your levels. Do you have a snack?

Liaquat No.

(*Peeps into her bag.*) What have you got?

Hema *moves her handbag away from him. From it, she removes a shopping carrier bag.*

Hema Here. Take your pick.

Liaquat There isn't much to 'pick' from, is there?

Hema Well you should've brought your own snacks, shouldn't you?

Liaquat I did. Last time. You told me off.

Liaquat *picks up the various contents and then drops them back in – apple, orange, ready salted crisps.*

Liaquat (*sighs*) I feel very, very sorry for you Hema jee.

Hema Now isn't the time to choose off a menu bhai.

Liaquat *gets excited. He fishes deep into the bag. He finds wrappers of little chocolate. He straightens one out and presents it to* **Hema**.

Liaquat Hema Malini.

Hema Yeah? What? My sugar levels drop occasionally, and I am compelled to eat sweet –

Liaquat 'Compelled' ha? –

Hema Which can I remind you is what you're going through right now. You'll be in a coma if you don't have something –

Liaquat Don't worry about me. I'll fight it off.

Hema You can't fight it off! (*Finds one last chocolate left. She gives it to him.*) Here, have this.

Liaquat You sure? Thank you! (*He munches it.*)

Do you have more?

Hema *searches her bag, then offers* **Liaquat** *an orange.*

Liaquat Oh look! (*Points in the distance.*)

Hema Kya?

Liaquat Do you see that over there? That moped? (*As he munches on it.*)

Hema Where?

Liaquat There, look.

Hema Fast food wala?

Liaquat When you're in despair, Allah gives you an answer. –

Hema No!

Liaquat You don't know what I was going to say –

Hema You're going to steal the chicken and kebabs from inside it –

Liaquat Tauba karu. I would never dream of stealing people's food. Nahi. We steal the moped from the boy and go to the mithai stop. It would take us there in . . . say two minutes.

Hema You can't just steal that boy's moped.

Liaquat It's not his. It belongs to them.

Hema He will get into trouble. You will get into trouble. I will get into –

Liaquat Listen closely, Hema jee. You go to the boy. I sit on the bike. You talk. Act like a sweet old budhi who's gone missing from the nursing home – 'kee hal hai, tussi teek ho'. Stand close to the boy. Grab his keys, rush back, throw them, jump on. We ride –

Hema Look at you. Sweating like a khota. What right do we have to take something that belongs to someone else?

Liaquat I'll give it straight back. I'm not a thief.

Hema You don't even know who that boy is.

Liaquat Exactly, he could be a horrible bloody bastard.

Hema Or maybe he isn't. Maybe he's a sweet gentle boy, struggling to make money for his family, and really needs this job, eh? Have you thought about that? We can't just play God and take something from him like that. Like people, eh? –

Liaquat Just like people?

A beat. **Hema** *stops herself.*

Liaquat What do you mean? Just like people?

Hema Eat the orange, bhai. You're still shaking.

Liaquat Nahi, nahi. Kya hai?

Hema It's just . . . sometimes I wonder if God really knew me, knew how small our time together was . . . how brief . . . before He ripped him from my life. Ignore me.

Liaquat Nahi, these things shake your faith –

Hema It hasn't shaken my faith –

Liaquat You wouldn't be human if it didn't.

A beat.

Hema It happened to you too?

Hema *waits for* **Liaquat***'s response.* **Liaquat** *nods, then struggles to correct the misunderstanding.*

Hema You only begin to know each other and then (*clicks finger*) they're taken from you –

Liaquat My wife. She –

Hema Every day I have to remind myself of the moments we shared because I'm scared one day I'll just forget . . . It was a long time ago. What right do we have to take the boy's moped? Eat the orange and let's walk back to school. Chal.

Hema *tries to pass* **Liaquat** *the orange. He doesn't take it. A beat.*

Liaquat Do you see those mangoes over there?

Hema Bus kar yaar

Liaquat Mangoes are zabardast.

Hema (*grips clementine*) I am resisting the urge to squash this in your mouth.

Liaquat Oh please don't. I can't eat clementines.

Hema *rummages in her bag.*

Liaquat And most fruits. It goes straight through me. But not mangoes.

Hema You're fussier than my grandson.

Liaquat *rifles his pockets.*

Liaquat Worry not, Hema jee. I'll take care of this . . . oh, where are my pesey –

Hema (*sarcastic*) Don't be silly, bhai, why would you have your pesey. (*Rifles purse.*)

Liaquat Nahi, nahi – put that away, you've already done too much for me –

Hema It's only pennies –

Liaquat Exactly. Stealing a mango is a lesser crime than a bike. She won't even notice. Look. Now's our chance, Hema jee.

Hema You can't go through life taking everything you want.

Liaquat Why not? It worked for the British.

Hema There's a cost to everything.

Liaquat You talk to the woman, I'll take the mango. I'll carry it on my conscience. Yours will be free, I promise. God will not punish you. He'll punish me.

Hema (*to herself*) He better reward me for testing me with you.

Liaquat What was that?

Hema Kuch bhi nai (*moves towards shop*) I'm paying for the mango. Haat-jao.

Liaquat *seizes her purse.* **Hema** *reaches for it.*

Hema Hey give me that! Give me my batwa.

Liaquat *evades her grasp.* **Hema** *seeks it.* **Liaquat** *reaches the shop.*

Liaquat (*to shopkeeper*) Asslamalaikum rahmatullahai wa'barakato.

Hema *moves towards it.*

Hema (*discreetly trying to get attention*) Give me my batwa back.

Liaquat (*to shopkeeper*) Kee hal hai puttar jee? Tussi teek ho?

Hema (*quietly to* **Liaquat**) Get out of there now.

Liaquat Ooh, sorry, I feel a bit.

Liaquat*'s eyes glaze over.* **Hema** *edges towards him.*

Liaquat I don't know what's . . . what's happening to me?

Liaquat *sways, losing balance.*

Hema Bhai?

Liaquat I feel really, really . . .

Liaquat *collapses to the floor.* **Hema** *rushes towards him.*

Liaquat *eyes flick open – he gives* **Hema** *a sneaky wink. He points to a mango.* **Hema** *gets angry. She just watches him. Lets him stay there. She's enjoying it.*

Liaquat Oh. Something's taking over me. Leave me. I'll be fine. Tell my children that I love them. Tell all the people I've wronged that I regret it, I hope they find it in their hearts to forgive me. (**Liaquat** *glances to see if* **Hema** *is doing anything.*)

Hema *smiles. Enjoying this.* **Liaquat** *points to the mango.*

Hema *looks closely at the mango. Apprehensive, pumped with adrenaline. She quickly takes one and runs. She holds it as if it's some explosive bomb.*

Liaquat Ooh, I feel so much better. Thank you puttar jee.

Liaquat *slips his flip flops back on and leaves.*

Hema *and* **Liaquat** *reunite. They giggle.*

Liaquat Wah. That's the rawest mango I've ever seen my whole life –

Hema You should've given me more time.

Liaquat I was on the floor for hours, my back hurts, the poor girl was gonna call me an ambulance. You took your sweet time picking a kacha aalm.

Hema I wish I picked up a watermelon instead. I know how I would break it apart. This isn't the season for mangoes, what do you expect?

Liaquat Did you see her face?

Hema (*trying to stop herself from laughing*) It's not funny.

Liaquat (*Essex accent*) Uncle, you okay? Uncle. Are you dead? D'ya want me to call ya an ambulance?

Hema Chup!

They burst into a giggle. **Liaquat** *squeezes the mango, moving it around in his hand.*

Hema What are you doing?

Liaquat Sweetening it up, aur kya?

Hema You can't ripen a raw mango. It's not ready.

Liaquat It will be.

Hema It will be, khatta.

Liaquat Nahi nahi – I know you're used to the Indian ones, let me surprise you with the more superior option –

Hema Superior? Achaa?

Liaquat *breaks it open. He passes her a piece.*

Liaquat Hahn. No matter how much they try, they will never ever be able to produce a mango quite as sweet and beautiful as a Pakistani one. Bismillah –

Liaquat *begins eating it.*

Liaquat Mmmmmmm.

Hema Pakistan has no monopoly over mangoes.

Liaquat Come on yaar, India has the call centres. We have the mangoes. Here, try this and see for yourself – sweet as sugar.

Hema Nahi, India produces over a thousand different types. Pakistan can barely reach forty.

Liaquat Because India hasn't found a single one yet that matches Pakistan – you just keep searching. And I wish you nothing but luck.

Hema Even the best ones you so desperately claim as your own were Indian once.

Liaquat We were all Indian once. (*Shivers at the thought.*)

Hema I mean our side. Our soil. You took some of our mangoes, re-labelled them as your own.

Liaquat Have some. Then, defend your country. Please.

Hema *gives in and eats it. It's nice, but she tries to hide it from* **Liaquat**.

Liaquat Nice?

Hema It's . . . sweet.

Liaquat What did I say?

Hema Eh. You should thank me for my choice.

Liaquat I should. Thank you.

Hema It wasn't much of a choice.

Liaquat It was kismet. The right mango was waiting for us.

Hema *sucks the mango off the skin.* **Liaquat** *does too. Like children. They sit in silence.*

Liaquat I also think my hands deserve some credit –

Hema For making it warmer, yes –

Liaquat And Pakistan too. We should thank Pakistan. Pakistan Zindabad.

Hema You woke up the birds and frightened them away with your . . . nationalism.

Liaquat No that's their excitement Hema jee – their souls are on fire because after all these lonely days, they finally found their own. These birds are apne.

Hema Birds don't fly that far, bhai –

Liaquat They fly entire continents, deserts, oceans for new homes –

Hema Hamaare jaise.

Liaquat Bil-kul hamaare jaise.

Hema Well if it's a bird from Pakistan, that means it's a bird from India –

Liaquat Nahi this can't be. Call out Jai Hind. See what they do. I'll close my ears.

Hema When you fly that high, everything looks the same –

Liaquat We look the same.

Mango falls onto **Hema***'s clothes. She tries to rub it off. It stains. Grabs a tissue. Stain goes deeper.* **Hema** *stops still, takes stock off the situation. The time. How things have changed so quickly.*

Liaquat Oh wow. Look. They're feeding each other. Isn't it funny how they feed each other through their mouths. I don't think you'd like that if you were a bird, Hema jee. You would refuse to be fed –

Hema This was a mistake.

Liaquat What was?

Hema I shouldn't have eaten it. My sugar levels are going through the roof. I can feel it.

Hema *wraps the mango piece into a tissue.*

Liaquat It's only a small slice. You'll be okay, Hema.

Hema (*almost to herself*) I haven't taken my metformin yet. (*Glances at her watch.*) Where's the time gone? I need to go – he'll be waiting for me.

Hema *searches her bag frantically –*

Liaquat Are you okay?

Hema We shouldn't have stolen the mango from them. It was wrong, what we did was wrong. How much did it cost? (*Searches for her purse.*)

Liaquat There's no need. Really.

Hema You still have my purse.

Liaquat Oh I'm sorry.

Hema Can you give me back my purse? Please?

Liaquat *takes the purse out of his pocket and returns it to her.*

Hema Thank you . . . You can't steal something from someone, no matter how small. Everything has a cost.

Liaquat You haven't done anything wrong.

Hema We're not little children – you need to stop acting like a little child, start acting your age. Sharam nahi aatee?

Hema *moves away from him.*

Liaquat I'll speak to the woman, explain the situation –

Hema No, please just stop . . . talking to me.

Liaquat Hema?

Hema Please, I beg this of you . . . I don't want you to talk to me anymore.

Hema *leaves* **Liaquat** *alone. He's taken aback.*

Eight

Liaquat *is in his kitchen. He holds the final ice-cream box of curry. Is he prepared to melt this?*

Liaquat

The last part of you . . .
is still frozen in an ice-cream box.
Suspended for just a while,
until I melt you, taste you again.
You slowly slip away,
but my hunger lasts a lifetime.
I'll starve, savour you,
(*stares at it*)
Karele.

Liaquat *tries to break off a small part. He pours it into the saucepan. The other half he keeps in the ice-cream box. He melts it in the saucepan. He leaves the curry to defrost and places his headphones on.*

Voice Liaquat ko karele bahot pasand hain. No one else likes karele like he does.

Liaquat *sits on the sofa and reaches for his wife's shawl and glances at the space beside him where she once sat. He seeks comfort* *in the shawl, holds it tight in his hand. He falls asleep – with his wife's tape playing in his ears.*

Meanwhile, **Hema** *is at home, she is doing some needlework to the insides of trousers.*

Hema I'm sorry I was late today beta. I should've told you where I was – time . . . time just ran away from me. I barely noticed it. Which is strange because most days, time is the only thing that I notice, but not today. Today I returned to the place me and your papa went when we first came here, where the ducks tread the paths like we do, and the birds nestle themselves in trees, feeding each other . . . and one place led to another, and before I knew it . . . I was lost. I couldn't find my way back – me – after all these years here – I got lost, and then I realised it . . . I tread the same streets, day after day, year after year, I go up and down the same path . . . but it won't happen again, I promise.

Hema *hums along to 'Kabhi Kabhi'. She can't get it out of her head.*

In **Liaquat**'*s house, a fire grows in the kitchen. Smoke rises around him. Alarm blares.* **Liaquat** *doesn't hear it. Fire grows.* **Liaquat** *is in danger. He doesn't know. The smoke begins to reach* **Hema**. *Both of them are indistinguishable from the misty haze. It consumes them.*

End of Act One.

Act Two

Nine

School classroom. **Hema** *is at the workshop.*

Hema Mrs Radcliffe has two packets of shortbread with her and today isn't even her cheat day. Her diet isn't going well. She is planning a relapse. She is timing this moment of complete utter indulgence for when she tells us to work with our partner to fill in a 'mood and food' diary, but time marches, and either he's late, or . . . he's not coming.

'Feeling stressed or depressed could be a root cause of emotional eating. If you're eating unhealthy food as a way of relieving stress, anxiety, you should try to replace them with something else. Work together to fill in a mood and food diary –'

(*Raises her hand.*) My partner isn't here . . .

And I think . . . I think you should call him to see if he's okay. She shakes her head –

'This isn't our responsibility I'm afraid.'

But his health is unstable, his levels aren't under control. He needs to be here.

'These workshops are entirely voluntary. It's his choice.'

Doesn't he, doesn't his health . . . matter to you(?) don't you care about him?

Silence.

But she doesn't say anything, so I sit back and watch the rest of the workshop continue to its finish, keeping my eyes on the door . . . but it doesn't open. Not once. When something blindsides you . . . you never learn to relax again. Not really. You fear the worse in everything –

I leave the workshop and as I wait, I see it . . . Mrs Radcliffe's bright red car.

She stops. A thought strikes her. Menace rises in her body. She steps back towards the school classroom. Apprehensive. Will she, won't she . . .

Mrs Radcliffe, I think someone's trying to steal something from your car. She rushes out of the room, I rush in. I look through her desk. Hundreds and hundreds of papers stacked up, it must be somewhere, his details, his address, something. Come on, come on. There's a list of names . . . Liaquat, Liaquat Aziz. Yes, yes, yes. I copy down his address. She comes in – oh . . . shit. (*To Mrs Radcliffe.*) Sorry. I just realised I forgot my dupatta, have a nice day.

Hema *storms out, breathes.*

Dear Mr Aziz . . . I hope this letter finds you well. I am writing to . . . request that you return to the Type 2 diabetes workshops. It was very disappointing to not see you . . . nahi . . . It's very important that you look after your health. I look forward to seeing you . . . nahi . . . Please make sure to attend the next one . . . Yours sincerely . . . Mrs Radcliffe.

Hema *seeks* **Liaquat**'*s house.*

Ten

Hema *arrives outside* **Liaquat**'*s house. She sees an overgrowth of weeds and plants – uncontrolled. She looks through the windows, and slips the letter beside the door, when the door opens. It's* **Liaquat**. *He's surprised to see her.* **Hema** *fills with quiet relief.*

Liaquat Hema?

Hema Mrs Radcliffe wrote a letter to you, and I volunteered to deliver it for her, (*passes it to him*) she was worried about you, she thought there was a reason you couldn't make the session, I told her there was nothing to worry about, that you were fine, that you would turn up to the next one –

Liaquat Thank you.

Hema Aap teek to ho na bhai?

Liaquat First class. Won't you come in for some chai?

Hema No, I shouldn't. My son will be here any moment.

Liaquat Acha teek hai.

Hema Maybe if it's just a short while.

This time **Liaquat** *wasn't expecting her to accept the offer.*

Liaquat Ajao.

Liaquat *and* **Hema** *step in.*

Liaquat *can hear his wife's voice on the tape player.*

Liaquat Ek minute, I left the TV on.

Next few beats play simultaneously. **Liaquat** *rushes into the living room and looks for the tape player. He can't find it. His wife's voice echoes in the space. Meanwhile,* **Hema** *is in the hallway. She calls her son –*

Hema (*over phone / to son*) Beta, I have gone to see conservatory-wali auntie. She had a knee replacement, remember. I won't be long. I'll get the bus home.

Liaquat *finds the tape player. He tries to switch it off. It doesn't work. He begins to panic.*

Hema *walks into the kitchen and sees burns on the wall. It shocks her. She opens the fridge. It's almost empty. She takes a few things out. Gone off.*

Liaquat *manages to switch the player off. He walks into the kitchen with the tape player in his hands.* **Hema** *quickly steps away from the fridge.* **Liaquat** *goes for the kettle. It boils.*

Liaquat Two sugars or one?

(*Breaks into a smile.*) I have sweeteners.

Hema Kya hua?

Liaquat *sees* **Hema** *glance at the burns.*

Liaquat Oh, the kids were making cakes and cookies –

Hema The kids?

Liaquat My grandchildren.

Hema Are they okay?

Liaquat They're fine. No one got hurt shukhar-hai.

Hema And you're okay?

Liaquat I wasn't here when it happened.

Hema I mean your health, your sugars.

Kettle has boiled. **Liaquat** *begins making tea. He finds it difficult and* **Hema** *notices.*

Liaquat It is as best as it can be, how is yours?

Hema Have you eaten? –

Liaquat Yes –

Hema When was the last time?

Liaquat I eat little bits here and there –

Hema Unhealthy snacks? Chocolate, crisp? Mithai?

Liaquat Nahi –

Hema Not whole full meals?

Liaquat *burns himself with the hot water.*

Hema Let me.

Liaquat Koi baht nahi.

Hema Please, here, sit.

They swap places. **Hema** *goes to make the tea.*

Hema Are you hungry?

Liaquat I'm full, I promise.

Hema You're shaking.

Going for the milk, **Hema** *sees the frozen ice-cream box in the freezer. She takes it.*

Hema Yeh kya hai? Ice cream or saalan? – (*Opens it up. She shows him.*)

I can defrost this for you –

Liaquat No. (*Grabs the box.*) My youngest daughter made that for me. She lives far away, I don't see her much, so I try to savour . . . her food. They spoil me rotten, you needn't worry, Hema –

Hema I'm not worried. We were supposed to work in pairs and fill each other's diabetes reviews you see, and I can't complete the whole review, my bit, without yours, but I think I have everything now, thank you. I should go.

Hema *starts to go.*

Liaquat No, please don't. Hema –

Hema After all these years, without your wife, you haven't learned to cook?

Liaquat (*hesitates*) No . . . I can cook.

Hema What can you cook?

Liaquat (*ponders*) . . . fruit chaat.

Hema Fruit chaat?

Liaquat Hanji.

Hema Achaa? You abstain from fruits, but you 'cook' fruit chaat –

Liaquat A good chef never eats his own cooking.

Hema I can teach you . . . how to make something.

Liaquat Now?

Hema If you'd like me to? I could.

Liaquat You would do that for me?

Hema No, you would do it for yourself. I would just show you how.

Liaquat That's an offer I can't refuse.

Hema You wouldn't need to depend on a single soul–

Liaquat What's wrong with that?

Hema What?

Liaquat Depending on someone.

Hema Roll up your sleeves bhai.

They both roll up their sleeves.

Liaquat What will we make?

Hema *opens the fridge again and stares at its emptiness, she scans the kitchen. Then glances outside.*

Hema Does anything still grow there?

Liaquat I don't think so . . . the kids maintain it. (*They walk into the garden.*)

Hema (*surprised/ironic*) Maintain it? What do they do?

The pair step into the outside. The moment drifts.

Hema You need to trim back those trees. You're stopping the sunshine pouring through them. Look. Do you see how the plants arch themselves towards it, seeking the light, the heat . . . Look. We can pick out all the vegetables we find and make sabzee –

Liaquat Sabzee?

Hema It's good for your health.

Liaquat With a couple of parathay on the side –

Hema Rotis will be just fine.

They begin looking for the vegetables.

Liaquat You're finding more sabzee than me in . . . my own garden, are you cheating? I won't have it. (*Competitive menace strikes him.*)

The next few cooking beats should play out physically, musically. Like a dance. They both look for vegetables. It becomes competitive and fierce. As they both go to take the same vegetable, their hands touch. It's intimate then awkward.

They take these vegetables into the kitchen. **Hema** *shows* **Liaquat** *how to chop the onions and chillies. He cries from the onions. He's clueless.* **Hema** *tries to stop herself from laughing at him, but he notices. She shows him how it's done. It's chaotic and fun. They turn to the vegetables and chop them too. The pot bubbles away. Steam rises from it, enveloping them.*

Hema *teaches* **Liaquat** *how to make the roti. They play with dough, like children. Kneading and kneading.* **Liaquat** *finds it difficult –* **Hema**'*s on his case. They add flour to it gradually.* **Liaquat** *cheekily flicks flour at* **Hema**, *trying to be discreet. She tells him to stop, frightening him.* **Liaquat** *rolls the dough.* **Hema** *uses this as moment to take her revenge.*

They place the roti on the hob. They watch it inflate like a balloon. Brown spots grow on it, before it gradually floats in the air. They watch it rise into the distance like a star they brought to life. **Liaquat** *is proud.* **Hema** *watches him. The balloon pops and disappears forever.*

Hema (*picks up the spice bottles*) Is this your handwriting?

Liaquat Kya?

Hema On these spices. It's very neat.

A beat.

Liaquat My daughter's. Is it ready to taste?

Hema *passes him a spoon.* **Liaquat** *takes it. He goes to taste it. She watches.*

Liaquat Something's missing. There's no flavour.

Hema 'Ha ha' very funny.

Liaquat I wish I was joking.

Hema Give me a spoon.

Liaquat *passes* **Hema** *a spoon. She goes to taste it.* **Hema** *takes it in.*

Liaquat What did I say? . . . kya hai?

Hema (*tries to calculate what she forgot*) Shhh let me work this out . . . garlic!

Liaquat Garlic?

Hema You forgot garlic.

Liaquat I forgot garlic(?!) You're my recipe. You forgot garlic, Hema jee.

Hema Are you going to get the garlic or not?

Liaquat *gets the garlic for her.* **Hema** *picks up some of the spices.*

Hema You were distracting me.

Liaquat Are you sure you know how to cook, or are you just some fraud? Sabotaging me eh?

Hema Nahi, when a cook teaches a non-cook how to cook, these things happen . . . my daadi said a part of you, your brain, goes to them. It's a noble sacrifice.

She passes it to him. They both chop them.

Liaquat Don't give me too much of your brain Hema jee, I don't want you to return home unable to cook. The children will be like 'aaj hum kya kha rahe hain', and you'll be like, um, um, Kellogg's cornflakes –

Hema Nice and fine, achaa, Kellogg's cornflakes! –

Liaquat Okay chef sahb.

Hema Better . . .

Hema *watches him chop it. She holds the garlic, smells it –*

Hema When I was a little, my daadi-ji would ask me to bring garlic with me whenever I came to stay (*remembers fondly*) I must've been six or seven.

Liaquat She wouldn't get them herself?

Hema Nahi . . .

A beat. **Hema** *doesn't respond.* **Liaquat** *notices.*

Hema She wasn't allowed . . .

Liaquat Kyu?

Hema . . . She was a widow. They thought those spices could . . . stir things inside you.

Liaquat Stir things?

Hema Hanh.

Liaquat Like what?

A beat.

Hema I don't know . . . feelings, desires, passions . . . make you feel things a widow should stop feeling, it's bakwaas. She had to use hing –

Liaquat Hing? yeh kya hai?

Hema Asafoetida. It gives the same flavour as garlic, but it doesn't –

Liaquat Stir things?

Hema Hahn, but I would smuggle them in my tiny hands – the garlic – I would break the bulb into small cloves and keep them buried deep in my palm, pressing tightly. My fingers would go red; my knuckles would go white – no one could find out.

Liaquat Did anyone? . . . find out?

Hema Almost, but I lied . . . my chest felt heavy. I hated lying.

Liaquat I don't think anyone enjoys lying, Hema jee.

Hema My ma would say 'Beti jub tum jhoot bolna shuroo karo gee to tumhein pata naheein ho ga ke kese bus karoon' – I would do anything for my daadi-ji even if it meant lying to the people I loved . . .

Liaquat She was a young widow? –

Hema Hahn. Daada died trying to protect his friends . . . during the days it happened.

Liaquat They were Muslim?

Hema And they were like his brothers. That was their home. He couldn't see them forced out of it.

Liaquat Allaah un ki magfirat farmai.

Hema She tried to do everything she could to get us to know this man we could never know, but it's hard . . . I see that now with my grandchildren . . .

Liaquat I'm sure they got to know him through you . . . Just like you got to know your Daada through her.

Hema (*touched*) I did.

Liaquat Your bond sounds special.

Hema It was. She was my best friend. When I was ten, I shaved my head so I could look just like her . . . Maybe it's then I doomed myself to relive her life.

Liaquat You cut your own hair?

Hema It was my friend, Rupinder. She held me between her legs and shaved it –

Liaquat Nahi. You're pulling my leg –

Hema Not a single hair remained on my head –

Liaquat I wish I could see what you looked like.

Hema My ma stopped talking to me for days, but it felt like weeks. Everything moves slowly when you're little. Her words still sting.

A beat. **Hema** *finds it difficult.*

Liaquat Sorry –

Hema 'You can't turn yourself into a boy no matter how much you try.'

Liaquat It must've been the shock, I'm sure she didn't mean to hurt you . . .

Hema But it was true . . . My ma sat me down and said . . . 'Hema, tum ub larkoon ke saath khelna bus kardo. Tum aurtoon ke saath raho. Tum aurtoon ke saath khaana banao.' She shrouded a dupatta around my head – 'you're turning into a woman' . . . I thought that I could just ignore it. That I could reach out and pull myself out of my fate . . . It was stupid of me.

Liaquat No it wasn't. Don't say that. It wasn't stupid at all –

Hema (*turns hob off*) It's ready. I should be going.

Liaquat Come and sit. I'll get some plates.

Hema I've already eaten.

Liaquat Kab?

Hema Before I came.

Liaquat Have a little. I still need to fill your diabetes review –

Hema We can do it next week.

Liaquat *pours the curry into the plates and gets the rotis.*

Liaquat You've done mine, and I didn't turn up this week, sit for just a while. I'll ask you quickly.

He puts a plate towards her.

Hema What are you doing?

Liaquat I'm leaving it right here, but you don't have to eat it if you don't want to.

Hema You can't tempt me like that. It won't work. Not on me.

Liaquat (*about to take the mouthful*) Bismillahi Wa Ala Barakatillah –

Hema *watches his reaction closely. The taste of the food hits him. He is moved by it.*

Hema Has the garlic added much?

Liaquat A great deal. It's . . . beautiful . . . thank you Hema.

Hema Nahi, it was you –

Liaquat Now, chalo, tell me about your health so I can fill this review.

Hema Nothing changed. It's . . . the same as it always was. Stable.

Liaquat Something must've . . . changed – have you eaten any meetha?

Hema No, not since the mango –

Liaquat Hema jee, you can't class mango as sweet. Mangoes are 'fruit' –

Hema With high levels of sugar. My levels have been creeping up ever since.

Liaquat It wasn't even a slice.

Hema It was more than a slice. I've had to introduce exercises into my daily routine to regulate my body again –

Liaquat What exercises?

Hema The ones Mrs Radcliffe was talking about . . . do you ever listen to her?

Liaquat Of course I do. Show me. Jog my memory.

Hema What? No!

Hema *sits down.*

Liaquat Tell me what to do.

Hema I'm not sure if you'll be able to do them.

Liaquat Achaa? Don't be so quick to write me off.

Liaquat *rises and begins stretching.*

Hema Exercising while you're eating isn't a good idea.

Liaquat (*burps*) Come on jee. I'm ready.

Hema Do star jumps.

Liaquat Yeh kya hai?

Hema Jump up and down, then widen your legs on the second jump.

Liaquat *tries it.*

Hema Nahi bhai, your feet actually have to come off the ground.

Liaquat *does it again.*

Hema Then widen your legs like a star.

Liaquat This is hard.

Hema You haven't even done one yet.

While **Liaquat** *turns and isn't looking,* **Hema** *tastes the food discreetly.*

Liaquat Nice isn't it? Zabardast.

Hema What?

Liaquat The saalan – you were eating –

Hema No I wasn't –

Liaquat I'm a good chef hanh? You're desperate to try my fruit chaat now.

Hema I didn't eat it.

Liaquat*'s exercise suddenly mutates into a Bhangra dance. Lunging.*

Liaquat Jhoot na bol. I caught you.

Hema (*laughs*) Ey! I wasn't eating. You're seeing things. It's making you dizzy.

Hema*'s phone rings.* **Hema** *sees it for a beat but decides to switch it off.*

Liaquat This is better exercise than star jump –

Hema You can't call that exercise. Yeh kya hai? . . . You can't dance without music.

Hema *reaches for the tape player.*

Liaquat *quickly seizes it out of her hand. He pulls a muscle.*

Liaquat (*in pain*) Aargh.

Liaquat *immediately lies face forward on the floor.*

Hema Are you okay?

Liaquat I need you to do something for me –

Hema Kya?

Liaquat You need to walk on my back.

Hema What? No! I will do no such thing.

Liaquat It will relieve me. The pain –

Hema It'll hurt you more –

Liaquat Aargh!

Hema *tries to stop herself from laughing.*

Liaquat Kyu has-re ho? Stand on my back.

Hema You've just eaten.

Liaquat Please! –

Hema You're gonna do ultee all over the carpet.

Liaquat I have a strong stomach –

Hema I'll fall on top of you –

Liaquat Hold onto the table.

Hema Okay, okay, Don't complain after this, okay? You're not allowed.

Hema *reluctantly walks on top of* **Liaquat***'s back, holding on to the table. She feels unsteady but tries to maintain balance.*

Liaquat Aah, that's good ahhh.

Hema Stop making those sounds please.

A beat, as silence lingers between them.

Liaquat You always hide your feet.

Hema I think you'll find everyone does –

Liaquat I don't –

Hema Yes, correct –

Liaquat I can see your feet right now.

Hema No, you cannot.

Liaquat But I can feel them, I can imagine just how they look as you press them deep into my back –

Hema Okay. I am getting off. Stop moving.

Liaquat Nahi, it still aches a little, aargh.

Hema *reaches for the tape player. She plays it. It's* **Liaquat***'s wife's voice.* **Liaquat** *reaches for it.* **Hema** *steps off his back quickly to avoid falling.*

Voice . . . kuch badal giya. Mere pe hasna nahi . . . mujhay lug rahaa hai ke mere dil ne pehli baar ye tasawwar kiya hai . . . ke mujhay us se piyaar ho ne laga hai. I think I'm falling in love with him.

Liaquat *stares at* **Hema**, *as she listens to the message. And then it stops playing. A beat.*

Hema Who is that? Is it your wife?

Liaquat . . . Yes.

Hema When she was young(?) –

Liaquat Hahn –

Hema Before she died?

Liaquat Nahi, she didn't die when she was young.

Hema I thought you said she . . . when did she die?

Liaquat Two years ago.

Beat. It sinks in for **Hema**.

Hema Oh. She has a lovely voice . . .

Liaquat Hema –

Hema I should go. My son will be worried.

Hema *puts on her shoes quickly.*

Liaquat Hema?

Hema Take care.

Hema *leaves.* **Liaquat** *is alone.*

Hema *keeps walking and walking and then stops still – perhaps an intense light holds her. She looks up. A child again.* **Hema** *smells* *her hands. They still smell of garlic. She tries to wash them frantically, but the smell doesn't leave. She keeps smelling them intermittently, panicked, haunted.*

Hema (*suddenly a child again – wracked with guilt*) Daadi jee didn't put any garlic or onions in the saalan, none, dil ki qassam. I watched her the whole time – mein ne khud haandi mein hing daalee thee. I promise . . .

Liaquat *eats the food that he cooked with* **Hema**, *filled with warmth.*

Eleven

School classroom. **Hema** *is sitting some distance away from* **Liaquat**.

Hema Mrs Radcliffe picked the wrong bag when she was looking for shortbread. She brought walnut cookies instead, except she's allergic to nuts, which means she will give them to the homeless man outside and he will say 'cheers love', and she'll return him a smile, and maybe for the briefest moment their eyes will meet. She's not been her usual self . . . too distracted by meaningless things, but that will change today. Her focus is back. Why did I make assumptions? See things that weren't there? Thinking she died like he did. Not everything revolves around you Hema, why do you keep opening your stupid big mouth?

Today, Mrs Radcliffe talks about 'long-term complications associated with diabetes' – 'your eyes have lots of important blood vessels which supply blood to the seeing part of the eye – called your retina – and when those vessels become damaged, they become blocked.'

Liaquat *tries to grab* **Hema**'*s attention.*

Hema 'And so, the seeing parts of your eyes can't get the blood they need in order for them to work properly, which means you can't see.'

Liaquat Hema!

Hema We each take our turns to have our eyes screened.

Liaquat *rushes towards* **Hema**.

Liaquat Hema! I wanted to thank you for coming the other day, teaching me how to make saalan.

Hema There's no need, really.

Liaquat I've repeated it –

Hema Kya?

Liaquat The cooking, your recipe.

Hema It's not my recipe. I can't claim it.

Liaquat I remembered the garlic too.

A beat. **Hema** *is unresponsive. Stoic.*

Liaquat Was there something I said which upset you? –

Hema Nahi –

Liaquat I'm sorry if I upset or offended you in any way.

Hema Don't be silly – you did no such thing –

Liaquat You left suddenly.

Hema My son was calling, and I hadn't noticed. My phone keeps turning on silent without me noticing, look. Silent.

Liaquat I didn't tell you when she died. My wife.

Beat.

Hema It was a misunderstanding. I didn't see things properly. That was my mistake.

Liaquat No, you thought she died when she was young, I should've corrected you, I wanted to but . . .

Hema You didn't –

Liaquat I'm sorry.

Hema Don't be. Please –

Liaquat I think I didn't want to talk about it – a part of me still can't – but I want you to know . . . why I didn't say anything then.

Hema You've been pushing it away? Burying it deep inside(?) . . .

Liaquat Hanh.

Hema You don't need to keep doing that. It's okay to let yourself feel it sometimes.

Liaquat *goes quiet.*

Hema It gets easier over time, I promise it does. It doesn't change. It stays the same size – that hole – but things grow and bloom around it eventually. Life moves on, but you can return and remember whenever you feel like it – I do – and sometimes you have no choice. That hole grows and swallows you up just for a while.

Liaquat She was my chacha's daughter . . . in our marriage, we had different jobs, responsibilities, but I never knew how much she meant to me until she was gone. It was like . . . a part of my body I never noticed, never felt, was suddenly cut off me. I have missed . . . so much Hema, I feel like I'm just chasing myself . . . trying to catch up with the kind of man I could've been and no matter how much I try, the past won't bring itself back . . .

Hema I'm sorry.

Liaquat Me too.

Hema Time only moves in one direction. There's no use in regrets –

Liaquat I never told her I loved her. I never uttered those words: I love you.

Hema Who does? Why should those three words weigh so much?

Liaquat It's not just words. I don't think she ever felt loved . . . by me, I don't think I ever made her feel my love.

Hema I don't doubt that she didn't know . . . I'm sure that she did.

Liaquat Hema.

Hema It's your turn. The eye screening. Mrs Radcliffe is calling you. Dekho.

Liaquat Oh.

Liaquat *gets up.*

Liaquat You will still be here when I come back?

Hema Where else will I be? It's not my turn yet.

Liaquat Teek hai.

Liaquat *goes to his screening.* **Hema** *watches him enter. Can he see how she feels about him? And then she turns and leaves the other way.*

Several moments later, **Liaquat** *returns to see* **Hema** *has already gone. He's alone.*

Twelve

Liaquat *is at home. He finally finds the VHS he was looking for.* Kabhi Kabhi.

Liaquat There you were all along.

Liaquat *slots the VHS into the TV.*

The recorded VHS fast-forwards itself. **Liaquat** *pours the food into his plate, sits to eat.*

Amitabh Bachchan, playing Amit, is being interviewed by Raakhee Gulzar as Pooja. Amit recites his poem to her.

'Sometimes the thought crosses my mind / It would have been delightful / Had life been spent in the soft shadows of your tresses.'

These words sink in for **Liaquat**, *as he tastes again the food that* **Hema** *cooked for him. The VHS frantically rewinds to the musical number where Amitabh Bachchan sings the title number in the forest. Music surrounds* **Liaquat**. *He doesn't know what to do with this realisation, the elation, the confusion. The balloon that appeared in the cooking scene reappears.* **Liaquat** *tries to seek it, but it escapes him.*

Liaquat
Kabhi kabhi mere dil mein khayal aata hain
Ki zindagi teri zulfon kin narm chhaon main guzarne pati,
Sometimes the thought crosses my mind,
It would have been delightful,
Had life been spent in the soft shadows of your tresses.

Liaquat *becomes restless. He doesn't know what to do with this energy. He stops.*

Liaquat
75 grams ghee.
250 grams sugar
500 grams milk powder
250 grams coconut
2 teaspoons . . . ground cardamom.
Hema, there was something I need to tell you . . .
I've been thinking about these past weeks . . .
These few weeks, in the time I've got to know you, I've felt . . .
I feel as though I'm falling . . .
I put the ghee, milk powder, coconut into a large pan.
I heat the tawa.
A small bright flame looms,
Like a scared life, bright beautiful.
the ghee slowly melts away.
I stir and stir and stir
I bring it to a boil,
It bubbles away
Pop-pop-pop

It sticks to the bottom of the pan,
but I scrape it off, before it can burn . . .
stay there . . . stuck forever
I stir in the cardamom.
It changes into a new colour.
A greyish green.
I pour it into a square tin,
It spreads into the corners, fills it far and wide.
I leave it to set and cool.
I slice through them,
Dividing, and subdividing them
into smaller parts,
I place them in a box
For her

Thirteen

While humming to 'Kabhi Kabhi', **Liaquat** *brushes ittar on his wrists and neck. He combs his hair. He smells his own breath on the back of his hand.*

Hema *is in the school classroom – ready for the workshop.* **Liaquat** *joins. He remains anxious the whole time.*

Hema Mrs Radcliffe eats her shortbread in plain sight, careless, unconcerned for the people who have to watch her munching away, as she talks. Her fears have gone. She can do just about anything. She's different. Hard. Numb. Hardness is better than softness. Hardness means you feel . . . less deeply.

'Some people with diabetes may develop nerve damage caused by high blood sugar. This makes it harder for the nerves to carry messages between your brain and your body.'

Liaquat *is apprehensive about approaching her. He suddenly decides to ruffle his neatly combed hair.* **Hema** *sees him.*

'The main danger of sensory neuropathy is the loss of feeling . . . this can be dangerous because you might not notice minor injuries, hurt . . . pain.'

And one by one, she takes us into the other room for a . . . 'foot examination' with the diabetic nurse –

Liaquat Are you going to run off again like last time? –

Hema I didn't run off. I was right here.

Liaquat I came back. You had gone. It's important you have these regular health checks you know.

Hema I do know actually –

Liaquat Even if you're too embarrassed to show your feet –

Hema I'm not embarrassed . . . It's the toes I have an issue with. Not just mine. (*Glares at his feet.*)

Liaquat This is why the gori's eating shortbread. If she must see everyone's feet, they can see her eat –

Hema Nahi, yaar. Gori has a foot fetish, she loves feet. Haven't you seen the way she looks at yours?

Liaquat You're pulling my leg –

Hema For her this is like eating popcorn to a movie . . . What is that smell? (*Coughs.*)

Liaquat Kya smell? Patha nahi.

Hema (*coughs*) Like someone's sprayed the toilet after they did their business – (*feeling sick, covering her nose*) disgusting.

Liaquat (*becoming anxious*) I think it's that budhi over there. I saw her spraying herself like this (*acts as her*). Hahn-na? Stinks. (*Wafts the smell.*) She should be more considerate coming here. Some of these buddai have asthma –

Hema *turns suspicious.*

Hema Bhai –

Liaquat Please . . . don't call me bhai.

Hema What else do I call you? Chacha-jee?

Liaquat Wah! Am I that old to you? –

Hema Baba?

Liaquat Nahi, nahi – Liaquat.

A beat.

Hema Liaquat?

Liaquat Yes, Liaquat is just fine –

Hema We near the end, and this is when you correct your name.

Liaquat Better late . . . than never.

A beat.

Hema Liaquat(?) It feels odd.

Liaquat My wife could never say my name. She found it hard . . . I think.

Hema I was the same with him. I still can't say his name. It feels . . . wrong.

(*Noticing the box.*) What are you hiding down there?

Liaquat Nothing (*pushes it away*)

Hema Is it . . . mithai(?) – oh my God!

Liaquat Can you sit back there please? –

Hema It is, isn't it?

Liaquat I wanted to bring it out at the end of the session, when everyone had gone.

Hema Why?

Liaquat It would be rude of me to bring it out in a type two diabetes workshop.

Hema That didn't stop you before.

Liaquat Fine.

Liaquat *takes out the mithai box. He opens it up – but without showing it to her.*

Hema Another box of ladoos eh? You won't ever tempt me to try one.

Liaquat What if it was something else?

Hema What do you mean?

Liaquat You said you would consider having a small bite . . . if you ever found it again.

Enough to keep your sugar levels stable you said.

Hema What are you talking about?

Liaquat Your beloved barfi . . . We never made it to the mithai shop, no matter how much we tried.

Hema It's from the mithai shop?

Liaquat Nahi.

Hema Because it doesn't exist, does it? I knew it.

Liaquat No, of course it does. What I mean is this box . . . This cardamom barfi. It's not from there.

Hema Then where is it from?

Liaquat It's from . . . me . . .

I made them myself –

He shows it to her. **Hema** *takes a look.*

Hema You . . . made them? For me?

A beat. **Hema** *is speechless.*

Liaquat You can't believe it can you? I made mistakes, I had to start again and again, multiple times, but somehow I got there. I didn't stop till they were perfect.

Hema They're not perfect, that's for certain.

Liaquat You haven't even tried them –

Hema Mein mazaakh kar rahee hoon. They seem good enough.

Liaquat I'll take that from you –

Hema There's so many. I said I would contemplate a small bite. That is not a small bite bhai . . . Liaquat.

Liaquat You have plenty to choose from, and the rest you can eat for a weekly treat. A hypo snack.

Hema They'll go off.

Liaquat Have them daily along with your metformin.

Hema I'm trying to put my diabetes in remission. I'll freeze them.

Liaquat You'll never touch them again. They'll stay there forever. They'll outlive you –

Hema Oi. Chupp kar. Nahi. I'll return to them whenever I need to be . . . lifted –

Liaquat Lifted?

Hema Hahn.

Liaquat Hema.

There's something I need to say . . .

A beat.

Hema Yes. What is it? . . .

Another beat, longer.

Hema You're worrying me, what's wrong?

Liaquat Sometimes I feel different parts of me aren't . . . connecting, and I can't feel what I feel when I want to feel and I can't stop myself from feeling, I don't know how to describe what I'm feeling, but sometimes the thought, the feeling plants itself in my head, and there's nothing I can do to shake it away because – I want to tell you that –

Liaquat *turns away from* **Hema**. **Hema** *waits for the answer. On tenterhooks, waiting for him.* **Liaquat** *is in a serious amount of pain – he clasps onto his chest. He doesn't know what's happening. It's a mild heart attack.* **Hema** *doesn't see this.*

Hema Hahn? Kya hua?

Hema *moves closer.* **Liaquat** *moves away from her.*

Hema What is it . . . you want to tell me?

Liaquat (*quickly changes tack*) I want to tell you how much . . . how much I appreciate your friendship. How much it means to me.

A beat. **Liaquat** *is heartbroken. Literally. And* **Hema** *too.*

Hema This was the thought . . . that planted itself in your head?

Liaquat You're the most wonderful friend and I don't think I've met anyone like you.

Hema Why are you saying it like that?

Liaquat (*realising it*) . . . I'm leaving.

A beat.

Hema Where are you going?

A beat.

Liaquat (*processing it further*) Home –

Hema Home? Pakistan? . . . You finally settled on returning? –

Liaquat Excuse me for a moment.

Liaquat *passes* **Hema** *the box of mithai.*

Please, try some.

Hema *takes the box. She is left alone.*

Liaquat *steps into the bathroom. He clasps onto his chest. He feels a heaviness and tightness. He moans in pain. He is experiencing another mild heart attack.*

Meanwhile, **Hema** *takes a piece of cardamom barfi from the box. She looks at it closely. She breaks a piece off it, almost about to bite it. But she can't allow herself to taste it. She returns the part of the barfi into the box. She gets up to leave.*

Liaquat *returns, recovered. He sees the box of barfi on the table. He sees the broken barfi. He removes it and places it in the palm of his hand. He tries to catch up with* **Hema** *as she moves away.*

Liaquat Hema! Hema!

Hema *stops and turns.*

Liaquat Here, you forgot your barfi. Did you try it?

Hema . . . I did –

Liaquat Kaisey tee?

Hema Lovely . . . it was lovely! –

Liaquat It was? –

Hema Yes, you've done so well. So, so well.

Liaquat It won't ever compare to the barfi your husband brought you.

A beat.

Hema It was lovely in its own way . . . Thank you.

Hema *leaves with the box.*

Liaquat *is on his own. He takes the 'nibbled' one and looks at it closely, presses his mouth against it. His eyes close. Kiss.*

Fourteen

Hema *is at home with specs on, doing some needlework on the insides of trousers. She occasionally glances at the box of cardamom* *barfi – but then looks away. She tries to resist the temptation. It becomes harder by the second.*

Liaquat *is at home, resting. He takes some tablets and stretches his body.*

Liaquat I have a question . . . Can a heart that's breaking – a heart not working properly – be used . . . for love? Can a breaking heart be . . . given to someone else . . . when no one can know how long that heart can stay beating, just breaking, until it stops?

Liaquat *hums along to 'Kabhi Kabhi'.*

Finally unable to resist, **Hema** *removes her glasses and her sewing. She rifles the box of barfi – seeks it out from where it's being hidden away. Like a child with a present. She opens it up – takes one barfi, looks at it closely as though it's a diamond and nibbles it. It melts in her mouth. Then she eats it whole. She smiles, on the brink of tears. It takes her back. Makes her feel good. She eats more. She laughs and cries at the same time.*

Hema All these years without a molecule of sweetness melting on my tongue. Where did they all go? All those years after you left me on my own. I was just a child, a young woman with my whole life ahead of me – instead I became your widow.

Liaquat *plays his wife's tape.* **Liaquat**'s *wife's voice rises, fills the space.*

Tape Kabhi kabhi jub mein sannatay mein bethee huwee hotee hoon, to mere des ki khushq mitti mujhay bulaatee hai, mujhay yaad dilaatee hai ke mein kahaan peda huwee thee, aur meri maut kahaan hogee, meree aakhree aaraam ga kahaan ho gee. Mein kahaan se aayee . . . aur meeri waapsee kahaan hai. I think about where I came from . . . where I'll rest.

It sinks in for **Liaquat**. *He is returning home.*

Fifteen

School classroom. **Hema** *is alone at the workshop.* **Hema***'s plaited ponytail has gone. She might've loosened it and brushed it at the end of the previous scene.*

Hema Mrs Radcliffe's shortbread has gone missing. She is convinced that someone stole it, that a diabetic exacted their revenge the final time they had to listen to a sugar-consuming woman rant about reducing sugar consumption. She feels violated, robbed of what she thinks she needs, craves.

She tells us to get into our pairs for the final time to discuss how far we've come, how we've improved, and what goals we want to set for the future, and then she will hand us each a certificate with our names on it, and we'll each stand in front of the group, while everyone claps their hands and I lose the will to live –

Mrs Radcliffe . . . my partner . . . my partner isn't here –

Liaquat Yes I am.

Liaquat *appears.* **Hema** *is surprised to see him.*

Hema You're still here?

Liaquat You didn't think I was going to leave before completing the course, did you?

Without my certificate . . . without saying goodbye.

Hema The flights won't be as cheap now with the school holidays, but then, it's one way, isn't it? Are you packed?

Liaquat Almost.

Hema When are you going?

Liaquat Soon. My nephew is getting the place ready.

Hema Make sure you order extra metformin from your doctor.

Liaquat I am seeing him tomorrow about this.

Hema And remember to spread them out in different suitcases, just in case one of them gets lost – you'll have enough to rely on –

Liaquat Teek hai. I'll do that.

Hema Achaa. (*To herself.*) Chalo.

Hema *gets up to go.*

Liaquat What are you doing?

Hema I'm not standing in front of everyone, while they clap for me –

Liaquat What about your certificate?

Hema It's just a piece of paper.

Liaquat You're sneaking out!

Hema I'm leaving early –

Liaquat You can't sneak out like this, Hema.

Hema She won't even notice.

Liaquat You're the only one who talks back to her, of course she will notice –

Hema I'll never have to see this woman again. It doesn't matter. None of this matters.

Liaquat We haven't even said goodbye.

A beat.

Hema Take care . . . Liaquat . . .

I wish you well. (*She smiles.*)

Hema *goes to leave.* **Liaquat** *quickly gets up to follow her. He's very heavy footed and slow (in pain, still recovering) unlike* **Hema**. *He causes her to blow her cover.*

Hema What are you doing? –

Liaquat I really wanted that certificate you know. (*They both run.*)

Hema I didn't ask you to leave, did I?

Liaquat Slow down! I can't run in these chappals.

Hema *slows down. They are now outside the school.* **Liaquat** *tries to catch his breath.*

Hema Are you okay?

Liaquat Hanji –

Hema If it's low again –

Liaquat It's not. I checked it on the bus.

Hema You do it yourself now?

Liaquat Why are you so surprised? (*Digs out his machine.*) Dekho.

Hema I was going to say. If it was, then I had just the snack.

Hema *unveils the packet of shortbread from her bag.*

Liaquat Hai meri Allah!

Hema *stifles a giggle.*

Liaquat You didn't?

Hema *nods.*

Liaquat No! How did you even . . .?

Hema She always does a poo before she starts. And it's not a quick tatti either. I could have eaten them all and gone down to get a replacement in that time.

Liaquat What's happened to you, Hema? –

Hema Kuch bhi nahi. That kutti would eat sugar before she told us to stay off sugar – why doesn't she stay off sugar, eh?! Beghirat.

Hema *eats the shortbread and offers the bag to* **Liaquat**. *He shakes his head, refusing it.*

Hema What's happened to you?

Liaquat I'm trying to get better.

Hema It's good to see.

Liaquat I need to.

A beat.

Hema I'm glad it all finally clicked.

Liaquat Because of you.

Hema Kya?

Liaquat *removes the tape player from his pocket and brandishes it in front of her.*

Liaquat Say a few words here.

Hema Kyu?

Liaquat So I can listen back and remember your voice. Go on.

Hema You don't need that. You can just put on a Bollywood movie and listen to her voice.

Liaquat Kaun?

Hema Hema Malini, aur kaun?

Liaquat It was a joke.

Hema Was it? I've been telling everyone that people mistake me with Hema Malini.

Liaquat I think it would be a mistake to compare you with anyone.

A beat.

Liaquat Now, are you ready? –

Hema Nahi.

Liaquat *presents the tape recorder again.*

Liaquat It's on.

Hema (*quietly*) What do I say?

Liaquat Anything you want! I don't mind.

Hema (*hesitating*) Ah . . . Uh. Hello. One, two –

Hema *takes it from his hand.*

Liaquat Oi.

Hema *ends the recording.*

Hema You can't listen to what I say now. You can only listen it once you've gone. Promise?

Liaquat Hanji –

Hema You promise not to listen before?

Liaquat I promise.

Hema *moves away with the tape player in her hand.*

Liaquat Where are you going?

Hema *speaks quietly into the tape player, recording onto it. We can't hear. Neither can* **Liaquat**. *A beat.*

She returns it back to him.

Hema I shall be going now.

Liaquat Me too.

A beat.

Hema I hope you have a safe flight.

Liaquat Thank you.

Liaquat Hema.

Hema Hahn.

Liaquat You know . . . There was something I was going to say last time. When I gave you the barfi.

Hema You said you appreciated our friendship.

Liaquat Yes –

Hema I do too.

Beat.

Liaquat Yes, yes, but that's not it –

Liaquat There was something else . . . different.

Hema Different?

Liaquat Something happened. Which stopped me from saying what I wanted, needed to say –

Hema What? What happened?

Liaquat My heart.

Hema Your heart?

Liaquat I felt sharp pains in my chest, and I thought I couldn't breathe, and I didn't know if it was my heart. Sometimes you forget where it is. Your heart. I did.

Until I felt it then. Tear against me.

Hema Oh no – I didn't know –

Liaquat I thought I was going to die. I thought to myself how mad I was to tell you –

Hema Are you okay? –

Liaquat I am now, shukhar hai. I had a PCI and in a few days I might need a bypass. How long I have left, only Rabb knows.

Hema You said you were going home?

Liaquat I realised it then. It's what's best. I can't have my body fly there in a cold box, Hema –

Hema Don't say such things –

Liaquat It's not good for the body. I want to go back the way I came. Alive. My heart beating in my chest. I need to set my eyes on my home one last time before I lay to rest in it.

Hema You'll be okay if you keep exercising, eating healthily. Managing your levels.

Liaquat It's not enough to hold back the tide. It isn't. I've made too many mistakes, Hema.

Hema Now's the time to start again. From the beginning.

Beat.

Liaquat That's what I thought.

Liaquat Hema –

Hema Just because your heart feels empty right now, after she died, it doesn't need to be re-filled, or replaced.

Beat. **Liaquat** *realises she knows how he feels. They share this moment.*

Liaquat But it's not being refilled or replaced, Hema. What would you say if I said to you that it's being shaken awake . . . that every part of this old thing is being filled fully, every artery, every vein is being felt, is hurting –

Hema I don't understand . . . (*She does.*)

Liaquat I realise what those . . . feelings mean. It took me a while because no one teaches you these things. You're taught how to become a man, work hard, marry, raise a family, support them, but –

Hema What are you talking about? –

Liaquat Love, Hema, I'm talking about love –

Hema Don't be silly.

They will fade . . . these feelings. We've lived our lives. They're finished. We're just waiting to leave.

A beat.

Liaquat But you felt them too(?)

Hema Stop fooling around.

Liaquat If we talk to our families, explain. They might not understand straight away, but over time –

Hema Understand what? Even I can't understand. How can I begin to explain to someone else what I can't even explain to myself?

Liaquat Why does it need to make sense?

Hema They'll be forgotten. These feelings. They'll be washed over, and you'll look back and laugh, and wonder what was all that? Why did it mean so much then . . . Look how big the world is. How small we are.

Liaquat I don't think I can do this, Hema –

Hema May God give you a long life and protect your health, and when our time is up, my ashes will be thrown in the river, and your body will be laid to rest in the earth of your ancestors, and there'll be . . . birds flying above us –

Liaquat Crossing continents, deserts, and oceans.

Hema Hahn.

Liaquat Humaare jaise.

Hema Bilkul, humaare jaise.

Liaquat What now?

Hema I go my way, and you go yours.

Liaquat Then what?

Hema We keep walking.

Liaquat We keep walking?

Hema (*readying to go*) I'll keep you in my prayers. Take care of yourself.

Liaquat Khudafis.

Hema *walks away.* **Liaquat** *stays still, looking at* **Hema**. *She glances back at him before she turns away and walks into the distance.* **Liaquat** *plays the tape player, clasping it against his ear. It's* **Hema***'s voice. What she just recorded for him.*

Tape (**Hema***'s voice*) Kabhi kabhi mere dil main khayal aata hain . . . Ke jaise tujhko banaya gaya hai mere liye

Hema *stops still. She turns to face* **Liaquat**. *Their eyes meet. She can't walk away from him.*

Lights snap to black. Darkness.

www.ingramcontent.com/pod-product-compliance
Lightning Source LLC
Chambersburg PA
CBHW041923090426
42741CB00020B/3464

* 9 7 8 1 3 5 0 6 0 3 3 5 6 *